Joke for t

MW00881088

Disclaimer

Do not remove this disclaimer under penalty of law.

For optimum performance and safety, please read these instructions carefully.

Void where prohibited. No representation or warranty, express or implied, with respect to the completeness, accuracy, fitness for a particular purpose, or utility of these materials or any information or opinion contained herein. Actual mileage may vary. Prices slightly higher west of the Mississippi. All models over 18 years of age. No animals were harmed during the production of this product. Any resemblance to actual people, living or dead, or events, past, present or future, is purely coincidental. This product not to be construed as an endorsement of any product or company, nor as the adoption or promulgation of any guidelines, standards or recommendations. Some names have been changed to protect the innocent. This product is meant for educational purposes only. Some assembly required. Batteries not included. Package sold by weight, not volume. Contents may settle during shipment. No user-serviceable parts inside. Use only as directed.

Do not eat. Not a toy.

Postage will be paid by addressee. If condition persists, consult your physician. Subject to change without notice. Times approximate. One size fits all. Colors may, in time, fade. For office use only. Edited for television. List was current at time of printing. At participating locations only. Keep away from fire or flame. Avoid contact with skin. Sanitised for your protection. Employees and their families are not eligible. Beware of the dog. Limited time offer. No purchase necessary. Not recommended for children under 12. Prerecorded for this time zone. Some of the trademarks mentioned in this product appear for identification purposes only. Freshest if eaten before date on carton. Subject to change without notice. Please allow 4 to 6 weeks for delivery. Not responsible for direct, indirect, incidental or consequential damages resulting from any defect, error or failure to perform. Slippery when wet. Substantial penalty for early withdrawal. For recreational use only. No Canadian coins. List each check separately by bank number. This is not an offer to sell securities.

Read at your own risk. Ask your doctor or pharmacist. Parental guidance advised. Always read the label. Do not use while operating a motor vehicle or heavy equipment. Do not stamp. Breaking seal constitutes acceptance of agreement. Contains non-milk fat. Date as postmark. Lost ticket pays maximum rate. Use only in well-ventilated area. Price does not include taxes. Not for resale. Hand wash only. Keep away from sunlight. For a limited time only. No preservatives or additives. Keep away from pets and small children. Safety goggles required during use. If rash, irritation, redness, or swelling develops, discontinue use. Do not fold, spindle or mutilate. Please remain seated until the web page has come to a complete stop. Refrigerate after opening. Flammable. Must be 18 years or older. Seat backs and tray tables must be in the upright position. Repeat as necessary. Do not look directly into light. Avoid extreme temperatures and store in a cool dry place. No salt, MSG, artificial coloring or flavoring added. Reproduction strictly prohibited. Pregnant women, the elderly, and children should avoid prolonged exposure to this product. If ingested, do not induce vomiting. May contain nuts.

Objects in mirror may be closer than they appear. Do not use if safety seal is broken.

Apply only to affected area. Do not use this product if you have high blood pressure, heart disease, diabetes, thyroid disease, asthma, glaucoma, or difficulty in urination. May be too intense for some viewers. In case of accidental ingestion, seek professional assistance or contact a poison control center immediately. Many suitcases look alike. Post office will not deliver without postage. Not the Beatles. Products are not authorized for use as critical components in life support devices or systems. Driver does not carry cash. Do not puncture or incinerate. Do not play your headset at high volume. Discontinue use of this product if any of the following occurs: itching, aching, vertigo, dizziness, ringing in your ears, vomiting, giddiness, aural or visual hallucinations, tingling in extremities, loss of balance or coordination, slurred speech, temporary blindness, drowsiness, insomnia, profuse sweating, shivering, or heart palpitations. Video+ and Video- are at ECL voltage levels, HSYNC and VSYNC are at TTL voltage levels. It is a violation of federal law to use this product in a manner inconsistent with its labeling. Intentional misuse by deliberately concentrating and inhaling the contents can be harmful or fatal. This product has been shown to cause cancer in laboratory rats. Do not use the AC adapter provided with this player for other products.

DO NOT DELETE THIS LINE -- make depend depends on it.

Warranty does not cover normal wear and tear, misuse, accident, lightning, flood, hail storm, tornado, tsunami, volcanic eruption, avalanche, earthquake or tremor, hurricane, solar activity, meteorite strike, nearby supernova and other Acts of God, neglect, damage from improper or unauthorized use, incorrect line voltage, unauthorized use, unauthorized repair, improper installation, typographical errors, broken antenna or marred cabinet, missing or altered serial numbers, electromagnetic radiation from nuclear blasts, microwave ovens or mobile phones, sonic boom vibrations, ionizing radiation, customer adjustments that are not covered in this list, and incidents owing to an airplane crash, ship sinking or taking on water, motor vehicle crashing, dropping the item, falling rocks, leaky roof, broken glass, disk failure, accidental file deletions, mud slides, forest fire, riots or other civil unrest, acts of terrorism or war, whether declared or not, explosive devices or projectiles (which can include, but may not be limited to, arrows, crossbow bolts, air gun pellets, bullets, shot, cannon balls, BBs, shrapnel, lasers, napalm, torpedoes, ICBMs, or emissions of electromagnetic radiation such as radio waves, microwaves, infra-red radiation, visible light, UV, X-rays, alpha, beta and gamma rays, neutrons, neutrinos, positrons, N-rays, knives, stones, bricks, spit-wads, spears, javelins etc.).

Other restrictions may apply. Breach of these conditions is likely to cause unquantifiable loss that may not be capable of remedy by the payment of damages.

This supersedes all previous disclaimers

any person acting upon the contents of this message without having had written confirmation.

This document originates from the Internet, and therefore may not be from the alleged source. If you have any doubts about the origin or content of this document please contact our Support Desk.

Moral:

This mail could have come from absolutely anybody masquerading as the sender, could have been read quite legally by the State under the RIP legislation, by the security services of any other state through which the data passes, by the sender's or receiver's employer on the pretext of protection of business interests, and read or altered by anybody working at any of the infrastructure services involved in its transmission. Given that internet routing is complex and adaptive, you don't even know who most of these parties are. Why not use encryption next time?

Jokes for the Modern Age
(And Then Some)

by Jo Kester

Table of Contents

Jokes for the Modern Age (And Then Some)

How do you milk sheep?
Bring out a new iPhone and charge $1000 for it.

I have 3 eyes, 6 heads and 15 limbs, what am I?
A liar.

I saw a sign that made me shit myself.
It said "Bathroom closed".

This is the third time my friends have agreed to attend a
Whitesnake concert and haven't turned up.
Here I go again on my own.

By legalizing Cannabis and same-sex marriage we finally
interpreted the bible correctly:

Steve Jobs would've been a better president than Trump.
But I guess comparing apples to oranges is unfair.

I invited my girlfriend to go to the gym with me and then I
didn't show.
I hope she gets the message that we're not working out.

Vegans think butchers are gross.
But people who sell vegetables and fruits are grocer.

1

I wonder what my parents did to fight boredom before the internet...
I asked my 18 brothers and sisters and they don't know either.

I couldn't join the KKK if I wanted to, my bloodline isn't pure enough.
Turns out my parents weren't even related.

If you masturbate after smoking marijuana....
Is it high-jacking or weed-whacking?

I wish I could be ugly for one day.
Being ugly every day sucks.

How do you break up two blind guys fighting?
Yell, "My money's on the guy with the knife!"

A woman is accused of beating her husband half to death with his guitar collection.
The judge looks down at her and asks, "First offender?"
The woman replies, "Nope. First a Martin, then a Gibson, then a Fender."

A man answered an ad that read "Hiring welders $18-$24 per hour."
When he arrived he was told he'd have to take a welding test.
He turned in 2 sets of welds. One was a great weld, the other was a mess. When the boss asked him why he did this he replied, "One is $18/hr, the other is $24/hr".

Jokes for the Modern Age

I once stayed up all night trying figure out where the sun went.
Then it dawned on me...

Genders are like the Twin Towers...
There used to be two of them and now it's a really sensitive subject.

I Will Never Forget My Son's First Words...
Where the fuck have you been for 16 years?

I asked my maths teacher, "Will we ever use any of this algebra?"
She said, "You won't, but some of the smart kids might."

Why are parents so bad at discussing sex with their kids?
When I was ten-years-old, I saw two dogs shagging in the street and asked my Mum what they were doing.
"Dancing," she replied.
The first school dance I went to, I got expelled.

"Son you're just not cut out to be a mime."
"Is it something I said?"
"Yes."

I went to the liquor store on my bike and bought a bottle vodka and put it in the basket on the front...then it occurred to me that if i fall or something happens then the bottle might break. So i drank it all right there. And its a good thing i did cause i fell 7 times on the way home.

To this day, the boy that used to bully me at school still takes my lunch money.
On the plus side, he makes great Subway sandwiches.

An Irish man frees a genie, and happy to be released from his confinement, the genie grants him 3 wishes.
The Irishman thinks about it, and says, "I want me a pint of Guinness that is never empty."
So poof a pint appears, filled to the rim with the rich brown drink. The man drinks it down, and when he places it back on the bar, it's filled up again.
"So, what would you like for your other two wishes, sir?"
"I want two more of these, then!"

An underage weasel walks into a bar.
The bartender says, "I'm sorry. I can't serve underage weasels."
The weasel says, "That's fine. I don't need something alcoholic. What else do you have?"
The bartender says "Oh, we have lots! We have water, pop, tea, coffee, smoothies. What would you like?"
"Pop," goes the weasel.

The doctor said my voice box is damaged and I may never speak again.
I can't tell you how upset I am.

I have a Polish friend who is an audio engineer.
and a Czech one too. Czech one too.

Jokes for the Modern Age

Dating is a lot like fishing...
Sure there is plenty of fish in the sea, but until I catch one, I am just stuck here holding my rod.

What does a pregnant teenager and her unborn baby have in common?
They're both thinking "Oh shit, my mom is gonna kill me..."

I keep getting hit by the same bike, at the same time and place, day after day...
It's a vicious cycle.

I have a phobia of over-engineered buildings.
It's a complex complex complex.

I searched google for "how to start a large fire".
52,000 matches

A man walks into a bar and orders nine shots of jaegermeister.
"Why are you ordering so many?" asks the barman?
"I just had my first blow job." says the man.
"Well shit, congratulations, have a tenth one on me!"
"Thanks, but if nine doesn't get rid of the taste, nothing will".

A bank robber pulls out gun, points it at the teller, and says, "Give me all the money or you're geography!" The puzzled teller replies, "Did you mean to say 'or you're history?'" The robber says, "Don't change the subject!"

During the last solar eclipse, I made a couple bucks selling fake eclipse glasses.
I'm not to worried though, those suckers will never see me again.

Why can't you fool an aborted baby?
Because it wasn't born yesterday.

I really love playing chess with elderly people in the park.
It's just really hard to find thirty two of them willing to do it .

My granddad was a WWII veteran. In just one day during the Battle of Britain, he destroyed 8 German aircraft, killing 32 Nazi aviators.
Easily the worst mechanic Luftwaffe ever had.

I gently slid her panties to the side...
....so I could fit her socks into the drawer

My buddy gave me a terrible thesaurus.
It was terrible.

A dad is washing the car with his son.
After a moment, the son asks his father, "Do you think we could use a sponge instead?"

If Snapchat has taught me anything ....
.... it's that a lot of today's teens look better as farm animals.

EMINEM: his palms are sweaty, knees weak, arms are heavy

Jokes for the Modern Age

WEB MD: Cancer.

The oldest computer can be traced to Adam and Eve
It was an Apple.
But with extremely limited memory - just one byte.
Everything crashed.

A 60 yr old Billionaire came to the Bar with his gorgeous 25
yr old wife!
Friend: "How did she marry you?"
Billionaire: "I lied about my age!"
Friend: "You said 45?"
Billionaire: "No! I told her I was 90."

My girlfriend and I were having sex the other day when she
looked at me and said, "Make love to me like in the movies."
So I fucked her in the ass, pulled out, and came all over her
face and hair.
I guess we don't watch the same movies.

This idiot on the treadmill at the gym just put a water bottle in
the Pringles holder.

An Englishman, a Scotsman and a Northern Irishman walk
into a bar.
The Englishman wants to leave, so they all have to.

I have a T-Rex who sells me guns.
He's a small arms dealer.

Jokes for the Modern Age

When does a joke become a dad joke?
When the punchline becomes apparent.

My neighbor asked if I knew anything about the missing clothes from her clothes line.
I almost shit her pants.

My wife just said to me, "Look at this, I've had this since we got married 20 years ago and it still fits me."
I said, "It's a fucking scarf."

Why do the French like to eat snails so much?
They can't stand fast food.

I knew a guy who survived mustard gas and pepper spray.
He is now a seasoned veteran.

Whenever I see a female bus driver, I'm reminded of how far we have come as a society...
Then I wait for the next bus.

An elderly man is stopped by the police around 2 a.m. and is asked where he is going at this time of night.
The man replies, "I am on my way to attend a lecture about gambling, hookers, alcohol abuse and the effects it has on the human body, as well as smoking, and staying out late."
The officer then asks, "Really? Who is giving that lecture at this time of night?"
The man replies, "My wife."

Jokes for the Modern Age

I went to a Halloween party dressed as a chicken.
Met a girl dressed as an egg. A question as old as time was answered...It's the chicken.

My neighbor obviously doesn't watch porn.
She asked me come fix her sink, I been here for an hour and I'm still fixing the damn sink.

A girl I know said the last time she had sex, it was like the men's Olympic 100m finals
I laughed, "Over in 9.5 seconds?"
"No," she said,
"Eight black men and a gun."

I was laying in bed last night looking up at the stars in the sky when I thought to myself,
"Where the hell is my ceiling."

We all know Albert Einstein was a genius...
... but his brother Frank was a monster

My son was thrown out of school for the third time this year for letting a girl in his class jerk him off .
I'm starting to think that maybe teaching isn't for him.

A man walks into a sandwich shop and looks at the menu board. It reads:
Grilled Cheese...$3 - Ham and Cheese...$5 - Roast Beef...$6 - Hand jobs...$20

Jokes for the Modern Age

A beautiful blond with huge tits comes to the register and says, "What will you have handsome?"
"Are you the one that gives the handjobs?" He asks.
"Yes I am!" She replies with a wink.
"Well wash your fucking hands. I'll have a Grilled Cheese sandwich."

North Korea now has a missile that can reach New York City, and I think that's really scary.
If it can make it there, it can make it anywhere.

Instructions how to fall down stairs:
Step 1
Step 2
Step 4
Step 14

Confederate statues these days...
[removed]

I showed the damaged remains of my luggage to my lawyer and said, "I want to sue the airline."
"You don't have much of a case," he replied.

I hate when you're over someone's house and they start asking you stupid questions.
Like "who are you" and "is that a gun?"

I accidentally ate a handful of scrabble tiles...
My next bowel movement could spell disaster.

Jokes for the Modern Age

I asked a librarian if she had a book about Pavlov's dog and Schrodinger's cat.
She said it rang a bell but she wasn't sure if it was there or not.

I have emotional constipation.
I haven't given a shit in days.

Saw the movie "IT" last night.
Far less "computer networking" and, so much more "murderous clowning" than anticipated.

If someone calls you a nobody, just remember...
Nobody's perfect.

When I see lovers' names carved in a tree, I don't think it's sweet. I just think it's surprising how many people bring a knife on a date.

How did Rhianna find out that Chris Brown was cheating?
She found another woman's lipstick on his knuckles.

A wife asks her husband, a software engineer, "Could you please go shopping for me and buy one carton of milk, and if they have eggs, get 6!" A short time later the husband comes back with 6 cartons of milk. The wife asks him, "Why the hell did you buy 6 cartons of milk?" He replied, "They had eggs."

I told my Dad he should embrace his mistakes.
He gave me a hug.

Jokes for the Modern Age

Apparently there is bi-partisan agreement, in Congress, that medicinal marijuana should be allowed for the purpose of relieving arthritic pain.
In other words, there is joint support for joint support for joint support.

Buzzfeed employee is diagnosed with stage 2 brain cancer,
Doctor: Number 4 will blow your mind.

Braille isn't that hard to learn...
You just have to get a feel for it.

A woman goes to the doctor. After a brief research the doctor tells her he has bad news, two pieces of bad news actually.
He tells her, "I'm sorry I have to tell you this, but you've been diagnosed with cancer." She responds, "Oh my god, no! And what is the second thing?" The doctor replies, "You have also been diagnosed with Alzheimer's." She responds, "Oh my god, that's terrible. Well, it could have been worse. At least I don't have cancer!"

So I've been talking to this cute 14 year old and now she's telling me she's an undercover cop.
How fucking cool is that for someone her age?

A man and woman were having sex and the woman was dissatisfied.
Woman: "You know, this wasn't what I expected when you said you were magical in bed."
*Man pulls out ten of hearts

Jokes for the Modern Age

Man: "And is this your card?"
Woman: "Holy shit."

A teenage girl brought her new boyfriend home to meet her parents.
They were appalled by his leather jacket, motorcycle boots, tattoos, and pierced nose. Later, the parents pulled their daughter aside and confessed their concern. "Dear," the mother said, "he doesn't seem very nice."
"Oh please, Mom," the daughter replied. "If he wasn't nice, why would he be doing 200 hours of community service?"

Dunno what this WiFi dude did....
But I've seen a ton of bars and restaurants demanding his freedom lately.

"Do you look at your wife's face when you are having sex?"
"I did once and she looked really angry."
"Why angry?"
"Because she was watching from the window!"

I told myself I need to stop drinking so much...
But I'm not about to start listening to some drunk weirdo that talks to himself.

I'm glad I wasn't close to my dad when he died.
He stepped on a landmine.

What has four wheels and flies?
A garbage truck.

We conducted an online survey....
...and found that out of the world's population, 0% of people
are Amish.

I started calling my toilet the "Jim".
instead of the John.
It sounds much better when I say that I go to the Jim first
thing every morning.

My wife found out I was cheating after she found the letters I
was hiding.
She got mad and said she's never playing Scrabble with me
again.

Arguing with a woman is like reading a software license
agreement.
In the end, you ignore it all and click "I agree".

An very attractive woman took a seat next to me at a bar last
night.
And brought it to a table of friends.

Wife: "There's trouble with the car. It has water in the
carburetor."
Husband: "Water in the carburetor? That's ridiculous."
Wife: "I tell you the car has water in the carburetor."
Husband: "You don't even know what a carburetor is. I"ll
check it out. Where's the car?"
Wife: "In the pool."

How does a red-headed man reach orgasm?
Alone.

A lady calls her butler into her room and says, "Jeeves, take off my dress"
He casually says, "Yes, Madam." and removes the dress. Then she says, "Jeeves, take off my underwear". Again, he says, "Yes, Madam." and removes the undergarment. She then says, "Jeeves, take off my bra." Again, with no hesitation he says, "Yes, Madam." and removes the bra. Then she says, "Now out of my sight! If I ever catch you wearing my clothes again, you're fired!"

Boy: [kissing girl on couch] "You wanna take this upstairs?"
Girl: "He-he, sure baby."
Boy: "Awesome! Grab the other end, and try not to scuff the banister."

Have you ever played quiet tennis?
It's like regular tennis but without the racket.

My neighbors listen to really good music...
Whether they like it or not.

Damn, girl, are you a math book?
Because you sure do have a lot of problems.

My favorite sex position is the WOW.
That's when I flip your MOM over.

Jokes for the Modern Age

Today it became clear to me that the letters 'T' and 'G' are far too close together on the keyboard.
This is why I'll never be ending an email with 'Regards' ever again.

I once persuaded my girlfriend to smuggle my coke through customs by sticking it up her ass.
I didn't know I could buy another can in the departure lounge.

Judge: "Why did you steal the car?"
Man: "I had to get to work." Judge: "Why didn't you take the bus?" Man: "I don't have a driver's license for the bus."

What does a clock do when its hungry?
It goes back 4 seconds.

Where does a spy sleep?
Under covers.

I entered a my pet snail into a race and removed its shell, thinking it would make it faster...
Unfortunately, it only made it more sluggish.

My Grandma Has Been Walking 5 Miles a Day Since She Was 57. She's 92 Now...
And we have no idea where the fuck she is.

I accidentally sent my friend flowers over the internet.
Whoops, E-Daisie

Jokes for the Modern Age

Why did the semen cross the road?
Because I put on the wrong sock this morning.

Two Scientists walk into a Bar
One says, "I'll have some H2O."
The other says, "I'll have some H2O, too."
The bartender gives them both water, because he is able to distinguish the boundary tones that dictate the grammatical functional of homonyms in coda position, as well as pragmatic context.

What's the worst thing about accidentally locking your keys in your car outside an abortion clinic?
Having to go in and ask for a coat hanger.

A boy is loudly praying, "God please give me a bicycle."
His mom asks, "Why are you praying so loudly? God isn't hard of hearing." The boy replies, "Yes, but grandma is."

I've been doing yoga for 5 years.
It's been a long stretch.

I was given MDMA and LSD tonight.
What a shit way to start a game of Scrabble.

A guy calls the hospital. He says, "You gotta send help! My wife's going into labor!"
The nurse says, "Calm down. Is this her first child?"
He says, "No! This is her husband!"

Jokes for the Modern Age

My husband called and asked if I could be naked before he gets home from work.
I feel awkward sitting here with his mother, but whatever.

Guys come on, we shouldn't give fat people such a hard time. They have enough on their plate already.

A child with an imaginary friend is normal.
An adult with an imaginary friend is strange.
And a group of people with an imaginary friend is called religion.

What clown has killed more children than "It"?
Ronald McDonald.

I just found out my best friend is a communist. To be honest, I should have known.
All the red flags were there.

Teacher: "Tell me a sentence that starts with an 'I'."
Student: "I is the..."
Teacher: "Stop! Never put 'is' after an "I". Always put 'am' after an 'I'."
Student: "Okay! I am the ninth letter of the alphabet."

What do we want?!
Low flying airplane noises!
When do we want them?!

Jokes for the Modern Age

NNNNEEEOOOOOWWWWWWW

In the UK we call them lifts, but in the US they call them elevators.
Because we're raised differently.

On September 11, 2001, I was in geometry class.
On that day, we learned you can remove one side of a pentagon by intersecting it with a plane.

I was fired for sending one of my students to detention "for being tardy".
Special education just wasn't for me.

If a stork brings white babies and a crow brings black babies, what type of bird brings no babies?
A swallow.

A teenage boy is getting ready to take his girlfriend to the prom. First he goes to rent a tux, but there's a long tux line at the shop and it takes forever.
Next, he has to get some flowers, so he heads over to the florist and there's a huge flower line there. He waits forever but eventually gets the flowers.
Then he heads out to rent a limo. Unfortunately, there's a large limo line at the rental office, but he's patient and gets the job done.
Finally, the day of the prom comes. The two are dancing happily and his girlfriend is having a great time. When the

song is over, she asks him to get her some punch, so he heads over to the punch table and there's no punchline.

Mom, I found a $10 bill today, but I threw it away, because it was fake.
"Oh, how did you know it was fake?"
"It had an extra zero."

We had random drug testing at work today.
The pcp was my favorite.

I saw a post on Craigslist that said: Radio for sale, $1.
Volume knob stuck on full.
I thought to myself, "I can't turn that down!"

Dad: "What do you get when you cross a tuna, a piano, and glue."
Me: "I don't know?"
Dad: "You can tuna piano but you can't piano a tuna."
Me: "What about the glue?"
Dad: "I knew you would get stuck on that part."

I once got yelled at for peeing in a pool.
Scared me so much I almost fell in.

Why did the chicken commit suicide?
To get to the other side.

I never knew how technologically advanced Moses was...

Jokes for the Modern Age

But today I learned he had the first tablet that could connect to the cloud.

Don't ever take a sleeping pill and a laxative at the same time. But if you do, you will sleep like a baby.

When i was born I was so mad at my parents. I didn't talk to them for two years.

A bear walks into a bar. He says to the bartender, "I'll have a............beer." The bartender responds, "what's with the big pause?
The bear holds up his arms and says, "Always had 'em."

I still remember my grandfather's last words. "Don't point that gun at me you idiot!"

I just realized that never is a contraction of 'not ever'. And blush is a contraction of 'blood rush'. And studying is a contraction of 'student dying'.

A police officer stopped my mom's car.
Officer: "First name?" Mom: "Frida." Officer: "Last name?" Mom: "Gomam." Officer: "So you're Frida Gomam?"
And my mom hit the accelerator.

I wasn't originally going to get a brain transplant... But then I changed my mind.

I have a pet tree...
It's like having a pet dog but the bark is much quieter.

Four engineers get into a car. The car won't start.
The Mechanical engineer says: "It's a broken starter".
The Electrical engineer says: "Dead battery".
The Chemical engineer says: "Impurities in the gasoline".
The IT engineer says: "Hey guys, I have an idea how about
we all get out of the car and get back in".

Two reasons I don't drink toilet water.
No.1 No.2

What's Gordon Ramsay's favorite Egyptian god?
IT'S FUCKING RAAAAAAA!

What do French men have that French women don't?
A oui oui.

My Granddad was a WWII veteran.
In just one day during the Battle of Britain, he destroyed 8
German aircraft killing 32 Nazi aviators. Easily the worst
mechanic the Luftwaffe ever had.

What does the bra say to the hat?
You go on a head, I'll give these two a lift.

I've got an inferiority complex.
But it's not a very good one.

Jokes for the Modern Age

"Do you think I reference dinosaurs too much when I write?"
I asked.
She was silent, like the p in pterodactyl, but it said everything.

My girlfriend was devastated to find out that my mates call
me 'The Love Machine'.
Because I'm terrible at tennis.

What's the name of the Mexican that loses his car?
Carlos...

I tried to submit a patent for a gold-plated butt plug.
But it looks like apple beat me to it. Turns out they are
already making overpriced toys for assholes.

I met two guys wearing matching clothing, so I asked them if
they were gay.
They promptly arrested me.

Doctor prescribed me LSD for my constipation.
Thought it was a strange until on the way home i saw a
dragon and shit myself.

I left two Justin Bieber tickets in my car...and some bastard
broke in and left two more.

I just heard that my grandma has finally stopped smoking.....
We can collect her ashes tomorrow.

Son: "Dad, a guy called me gay at the school today."
Dad: "Punch him in the face."

Jokes for the Modern Age

Son: "But he is so cute."

Two blondes are going to Disney Land. At the turn off, they see a sign saying "Disneyland left"
They went home crying.

Somebody actually complimented me on my driving today. They left a little note on the windscreen, it said 'Parking Fine.'
So that was nice.

Today I donated a watch, a phone and my wallet to a poor guy...
You can't know the happiness I felt as I saw him put his knife back in his pocket.

I told my friend people keep accidentally asking me to buy meat for them.
He asked: "By mistake?"
I said: "Oh come on, not you too!"

I just flew in from Chernobyl...
And boy are my arms legs.

Build a man a fire and you'll keep him warm for a night... set a man on fire and you'll keep him warm for the rest of his life.

I bought my 19 year old daughter a new bed for when she goes off to university. She was undecided about whether she wanted to keep it. I told her to sleep on it.

Life is like a penis.
It's all relaxed freely hanging, and then a woman comes and makes it hard.

If the USSR suddenly came back together...
... it should be called the Soviet Reunion.

Just found out that 'Aaarrrrgggghhh' is not a real word.
I can't even tell you how angry I am.

Why didn't the sun go to college?
It already had a million degrees.

Two men are playing golf. One of them is about to take a swing when a funeral procession appears on the road next to the course. He stops mid-swing, takes off his cap, closes his eyes, and bows his head in contemplation.
His opponent comments, "That must be the most touching thing I've ever seen. You are a very feeling man." The man, recovering himself, replies, "Yeah, well we were married 35 years."

What do you call a communist sniper?
A marxman.

What's the difference between a politician and a flying pig?
The letter F.
I went for a job interview at EA Games today.
The interviewer said to me, "The second part of your resume is missing."

Jokes for the Modern Age

I said, "For the second part, you have to pay $20."

I told two twins their matching outfits are cute...
"Did your mom buy you matching clothes?" I asked politely.
To which they answered, "We're not twins and could we see
your license and registration please."

Talk Like A Pirate Day...
How the fuck am I supposed to learn Somali?

What do gay horses eat?
Horse dick.

Some say that if you play Nickelback backwards you'll hear
Satan.
Even worse, if you play it forwards you'll hear Nickelback.

I was breastfed until 3.
But enough about my day, how was yours?

My girlfriend's parents called me a disgusting creep, just
because I am 36 and she is 24.
What a horrible thing to say on our son's 10th birthday party.

I was forced to swallow purple food color.
I feel violated.

Imagine if America switched from pounds to kilograms
overnight...
There would be mass confusion.

"There's no 'I' in team"
"But there's a whole lot of 'U' in shut the fuck up"

An idiot has a mirror in his closet.
He wakes up one night and opens the closet and he sees himself. Scared, he quickly calls the cops.
"Police! There's a burglar in my closet, come quickly!"
A police man arrives at the idiots house and opens the closet and finds the mirror. He takes a step back and slaps the idiot as hard as he can.
"Why did you call me when you already had a policeman inside?!"

"I'm going to punch your house until you come out and talk to me!"
~ Guy who invented 'knocking'.

What did the boy with no hands get for Christmas?
GLOVES! Nah, just kidding... He still hasn't unwrapped his present.

The husband and the wife were having dinner at a fancy restaurant.
A few minutes later, the dinner was served.
Husband: "The food looks great. Let's eat."
Wife: "But honey, you always say a prayer before eating at home."
Husband: "That's at home, sweetie. I'm sure the chef here knows how to cook."

I hate it when engineering students refer to themselves as engineers...
Like you don't see med students calling themselves doctors or arts students calling themselves unemployed.

I remember once, when my dad gave me money to pay the electricity bill, but instead I bought a raffle ticket for a brand new car. When I got home, I explained to my dad what I did, and he beat the crap out of me. But the next day,when my dad woke up and opened the door, outside my house was a brand new car. We all cried. Especially me, because the car was from the electricity company. They were there to cut off the electricity. My dad beat the crap out of me again.

Son: "Dad, Am I adopted"?
Dad: "Not yet. We still haven't found anyone who wants you."

I got fired from my job at the library.
Apparently the book on women's rights doesn't belong in the fiction section.

Co-worker asked me, "If Batman, who is a regular human, but with gadgets, teamed up with Superman, who has supernatural powers, and they fought against Iron Man, another regular human with gadgets, who teamed up with Thor, who has super powers, who would be the winners?"
"Your parents when you move out."

I never knew how technologically advanced Moses was.

But today I learned he had the first tablet that could connect to the cloud.

A 70 year old man went for a sperm test. The Doctor gave him a bottle to collect sperm.
The next day, the man came with the empty bottle and said he tried with his left hand, and then his right hand. Then his wife tried with her left hand and right hand. Then his daughter-in-law tried with both hands & mouth. Then the neighbor's wife & daughter tried the same way...but could not open the damn bottle.

A plumber fixes a damaged pipe in a doctor's house and asks for 200 dollars. Doctor says to him: "Even I don't make so much money in such a short period and I'm a doctor".
And the plumber says, "I know sir. I used to be a doctor myself."

Iron Man is technically a Female

So this guy at college keeps calling me a flamingo.
One of these days I'm going to put my foot down.

Girl: "Come over"
Guy: "I'm coming over."
Girl: "We should stop using walkie talkies in bed, over."

What's the difference between a car tire and 365 used condoms?
One's a Goodyear, one's a great year.

Jokes for the Modern Age

"Indecisive" is my favorite word.
Actually, no it isn't.

Why did the hobbit set his cell phone to vibrate?
He was afraid the ring would give him away.

It's impossible to please women.
Even at your wedding, you are not the best man.

What's worse than finding a worm in your apple?
Cutting your toe off with an ax.

I never wanted to believe my dad was stealing things at his
job as a road worker.
But when I got home, all the signs were there.

Girlfriend said that she slept with 61 men before.
I doubt it, but she insisted that I was her sixty-second man.

How does an Indian girl tell her family she will be wearing a
Western dress to her wedding?
"Sorry, not Sari."

I suggested to my wife that she'd look sexier with her hair
back..
..which is apparently an insensitive thing to say to a cancer
patient.

I beat my wife and she immediately divorced me.
Some people take Monopoly way too seriously.

Jokes for the Modern Age

How do you confuse an Apple user?
Give them options.

A vegan, feminist and a famous rapper walk in a bar
I only knew because they told me 10 times.

I only know 25 letters...
I don't know Y.

As an airplane is about to crash, a female passenger jumps up
frantically and announces, "If I'm going to die, I want to die
feeling like a woman." She removes all her clothing and asks,
"Is there someone on this plane who is man enough to make
me feel like a woman?" A man stands up, removes his shirt
and says, "Here, iron this!"

My girlfriend just sent me a message saying:
"myspacebarbrokecanyoucomeoverandgivemeanalternative"
Does anybody know what 'ternative' means?

I got fired from PC World today.
A guy came in the store and asked me what was the best thing
for finding your ancestors.
"Probably a shovel" was not the right answer.

I covered all my weapons in glue.
I questioned it at first, but I decided to stick to my guns.

I work in a prison, and when people ask me if I enjoy my job,
I tell them that it has it's pros and cons.

My wife said I'm lazy.
I almost told her how wrong she is.

20 men walk into a bar.
Worst game of limbo I've ever seen.

TIL cow tipping is an urban myth.
Apparently, the farmers just pay them a competitive wage.

My ceiling may not be the best ceiling in the world. But it's up there.

A woman gets on a bus with her baby. The bus driver says, "That's the ugliest baby that I've ever seen. Ugh!" The woman goes to the rear of the bus and sits down, fuming. She says to a man next to her, "The driver just insulted me!" The man says, "You go right up there and tell him off – go ahead, I'll hold your monkey for you."

In the beginning, there was nothing...
Then God says "let there be light". Now there was still nothing, but at least you can see it.

I hate when homeless people shaking their cup of coins at me. Like, yeah, I know you have more money than me, but you don't need to rub it in.

I was in a bar last night when a waitress screamed...

"Does anyone know CPR?" "I know all the letters of the alphabet." I shouted back. Everyone laughed.........well except this one guy.

I get so angry when I see someone with their wallet chained to their belt.

I just can't take it.

A man who lived in a block of apartments thought it was raining and put his head out the window to check. As he did, so a glass eye fell into his hand. He looked up to see where it came from, just in time to see a young woman looking down. "Is this yours?" He asked. She said, "Yes, could you bring it up?" and the man agreed. On arrival she was profuse in her thanks and offered the man a drink. As she was very attractive, he agreed. Shortly afterwards she said, "I'm about to have dinner. There's plenty. Would you like to join me?" He readily accepted her offer and both enjoyed a lovely meal. As the evening was drawing to a close the lady said, "I've had a marvelous evening. Would you like to stay the night?" The man hesitated then said, "Do you act like this with every man you meet?" "No," she replied, "Only those who catch my eye."

An inventor shows his friend the first knife ever.
His friend says, "Wow! That's the best thing since bread."
The inventor says, "Well, I'm about to blow your mind."

My motto in life is to always give 100%.
It does make blood donation quite tricky.

I wanted to be an astronaut when I was a kid,
but my mom told me the sky is the limit.

My wife once asked me if I would ever sleep with her sister if
we split up.
"Which sister?" is not the correct answer.

I'm all for jokes, but jokes about sexually abusing mentally
handicapped people?
That's fucking retarded.

I came home from work last night and told my wife that I've
been given a huge promotion at work, which means I get my
own office, and I get to employ my own private secretary.
"Well, you'd better hire someone who's a bit old, fat and
ugly," she said. "I don't want you choosing someone who
you're going to be tempted to have sex with".
"That's fair enough" I replied "When can you start?"

My wife is so ugly...
she walked past the walrus enclosure at Sea World, and her
iPhone X unlocked itself.

So I broke my waterproof speaker by throwing it into a pool.
I filed a request for a new speaker, but the company
responded, "it's not our fault the pool was empty".

I tried asking a Ouija Board for the name of my future wife.

The planchette kept moving from H to A and back. What kind of name is Hahaha?

Sherlock Holmes is inspecting a bed. He says to Watson, "This bed is missing something." Watson replies "No sheet Sherlock."

To the guy that found my empty wallet.
I don't know how to repay you.

I went to a pub last night and saw a fat chick dancing on a table. I said, "Nice legs."
The girl giggled and said with a smile, "Do you really think so?"
I said "Definitely! Most tables would have collapsed by now."

I'm single by choice... just not my choice.

You can't run through a campsite.
You can only ran because it's past tents.

What's the name of the fastest Chinese online game player?
Lo Ping

Why do thieves prefer to steal Android phones over iPhones?
Because they like to Hangout and not FaceTime.

My girlfriend accidentally discovered a way to get long lashes, instantly.

Jokes for the Modern Age

By showing a bit of ankles in Saudi Arabia.

Heaven is where the police are British, the cooks are French, the mechanics German, the lovers Italian and it's all organized by the Swiss.

Hell is where the chefs are British, the mechanics French, the lover's Swiss, the police German and it's all organized by the Italians.

Tesla released a car air freshener last week.
They call it Elon's Musk.

A 60 year old Billionaire goes to the bar...
...with his gorgeous 25 year old wife!
The bartender asks him, "How did she marry you?"
The billionaire replies, "I lied about my age!"
The bartender then says, "You said 45?"
To which the billionaire replies, "No! I said 90!"

I have a dog with no legs. I call him cigarette...
... every night I take him out for a drag.

Little Johnny goes to his grandfather and asks him to croak like a frog.
"Why, sure Johnny. Croak", says grandfather. "Yaaaaay", exclaimed Johnny. Confused, grandfather asks what's so exciting. "Papa says we're going to be rich when you croak!", replies johnny.

Jokes for the Modern Age

News just in:
Someone has been killed with a starter pistol !!!
Police think it might be race related.

My girlfriend didn't believe me when I said I have the body of
20 year old.
Her opinion changed when I opened the freezer.

Viagra is a gateway drug.
It leads to harder things.

I have a fear of speed bumps.
I'm slowly getting over it.

I was sitting in a bar one day, and two really large women
came in, talking in an interesting accent.
So I said, "Cool accent. Are you two ladies from Ireland?"
One of them snarled at me, "It's Wales, dumbo!"
So I corrected myself, "Oh, right. So are you two whales from
Ireland?"
That's about as far as I remember.

I watched director's cut of a porn film...
At the end he actually fixed the washing machine.

My Girlfriend left a note on the refrigerator that said: "This
isn't working. Goodbye."
I opened the refrigerator and it was working fine. WTF?

An old dying man invites 3 of his friends to his deathbed and asks a favor.

He says, "We've been as brothers for longer than I can remember, and while I was not rich in life, I would like to bring some wealth with me as I die. If you could each leave $5,000 in my coffin, it would bring me great peace."

The three men saw no fault in this, as they were all very rich, and all upstanding members of their respective communities.

Jim was a devout, aging Catholic, and he brought the five thousand in large bills, so as not to occupy much space in the coffin. He later told the members of his congregation, and oh how they lauded him on his selflessness to ease the mind of a dying friend.

Michael was a converted Muslim, and he feared that the dead had no use for paper money, so he converted the five thousand into gold for his friend, leaving the ingots next to the bills. He felt a great warmth inside of him, a feeling that can only be brought about by a good, charitable deed.

David was born Jewish, but wasn't so devout as many of his colleagues. He refused to buck off the stereotype and worked as a moneylender, a loan agent. Because of this, he understood how exchange rates worked and how trying to convert 3 different types of money to one may be hard for a man with little experience handling cash. Therefore, he wrote a check for fifteen thousand dollars, and took the gold and bills as change. He left his friend's side with such a great smile, he must have known the time he'd saved him in the afterlife.

What do you get when you cross goat DNA with human DNA?

Jokes for the Modern Age

You get kicked out of the petting zoo.

I tried rocking my newborn daughter to sleep.
Apparently she isn't a big Zeppelin fan.

A little boy returning home from his first day at school said to his mother, "Mom, what's sex?" His mother, who believed in all the most modern educational theories, gave him a detailed explanation, covering all aspects of the tricky subject. When she had finished, the little lad produced an enrollment form which he had brought home from school and said, "Yes, but how am I going to get all that into this one little square?"

"What does the word 'gay' mean?", asked a son his father.
"It means 'happy'", replied the father.
"Oh," contested the son, "so you are gay then?"
"No, son, I have a wife."

I told my girlfriend that if she wanted her Hershey's bar, she had to bark like a dog.
After she did it, I proceeded to eat it, explaining that chocolate wasn't good for dogs.

I remember the last words my grandpa said before he kicked the bucket...
"Hey, how far do you reckon I could kick this bucket?"

Why are North Korean weekends so lame?
Because there's only one party.

My doctor told me to eat more Taco Bell.

Well, actually he said, "less McDonald's", but I'm pretty sure I know what he meant.

What did the physicist say to the man who was about to jump off a building?

"Don't do it! You have so much potential."

I just found my old Nokia and connected it with my power bank.

The power bank is now fully charged again.

I just found out I'm being followed!

My girlfriend told me she's been seeing people behind my back.

Two guys were drinking at the bar...

Bubba: "You know, I've never understood what dilemma is.."

Jimmy: "Let me give you an example. Imagine you wake up in a bed with two people next to you.

To your left is an incredibly beautiful woman willing to have you, and to your right is a very horny gay man."

Bubba: "So where's the dilemma?"

Jimmy: "To whom do you turn your back?"

I phoned my wife earlier, and asked her if she wanted me to pick up fish and chips on my way home from work, but she just put the phone down on me.

I think she still regrets letting me name the twins.

What can you say about your car, but not your girlfriend?
She died last week, but I still use some of the parts.

In a certain tribe, in which polygamy was practiced, a married man's standing in the tribe depended upon the combined weight of his wives - the greater the combined weight, the more important was the man. Every year, on weighing day and according to custom, the married men would stand their wives on neatly spread animal skins. Then the chief of the tribe would come around with a crude seesaw and balance the wives of one man, against those of another, in order to determine the relative importance of the men. Now Gog had only one wife, who was very heavy, while Gug had two much slenderer wives. And all year the two men argued as to who was the more important. When weighing day arrived, Gog placed his wife on a large hippopotamus skin, and Gug placed his wives on two small gazelle skins.

When the weighing was performed, it was found that Gog's wife exactly balanced against the two wives of Gug. Thus, it turned out, that the two men were equally important, since, by the chief's ruling, "the squaw on the hippopotamus is equal to the sum of the squaws on the other two hides."

How do you milk sheep?
With iPhones.

Subway is a lot like prostitution.
You're paying someone else to do your wife's job.

It was my first day at a new school.
When I arrived, I wanted to make sure nobody would pick on me, so I walked up to the captain of the football team and punched him in the face. He fell to the ground, unconscious. From that day forward, everyone knew not to mess with the new principal.

Why should you never marry a tennis player?
Because to tennis players, love means nothing.

The volume of a pizza with thickness a and radius z =
pi * z * z * a.

"Poor old fool," thought the well-dressed gentleman, as he watched an old man fish in a puddle outside a pub. So he invited the old man inside for a drink. As they sipped their whiskeys, the gentleman thought he'd humor the old man and asked, "So how many have you caught today?"
The old man replied, "You're the eighth one."

What do you call a drunk women?
An Uber so she can get home safely.

A blind guy walks into a bar with his seeing eye dog...
The bartender begins to greet him, but is shocked to see the man grab the dog by the tail, and swing it around his head.
"What the fuck are you doing?!" the barman cries. The blind man shrugs. "Just having a look around."

What's the difference between E.T. and a refugee?

Jokes for the Modern Age

E.T. learned English and wanted to go home.

Accidentally sent someone flowers over the internet.
Whoops e-daisies.

I scared the postman today by going to the door completely naked…
I'm not sure what freaked him out more – my naked body, or the fact that I knew where he lived.

A polar bear walks into a bar. Bartender says, "What can I get you?" The bear replies, "I'd like a gin......... and tonic"
Bartender asks, "Why the big pause?" The polar bear looks at his hands, turning them back and forth. "I don't know, my dad had 'em too."

I was arguing with a flat Earth believer...
We argued about how many members the flat Earth community had. He said. "We have members all around the globe".

My Dad had a headache the other day so I asked if he needed any pills.
He said "The only pills that could have stopped this head ache should have been taken 16 years ago."
My girlfriend told me to take the spider out instead of killing it....
We went out and had some drinks. Cool guy. Wants to be a web developer.

Jokes for the Modern Age

Yesterday, I found out I was colorblind.
The news came out of the green.

I just learned the movie Starship Troopers was never adapted
into a successful video game because...
...bugs.

A pirate goes to a doctor worried that the moles on his back
might be cancerous. The doctor inspects them. "It's ok", he
says. "They're benign." The pirate replies, "Check 'em again
matey. I think there be at least ten!"

How long is a Chinese name.
No really it is.

I bought a trash compactor for my ex-wife.
Or, as Victoria Secret calls it - a corset.

A husband and wife have four sons. The oldest three are tall
with red hair and light skin, while the youngest son is short
with black hair and dark eyes. The husband was on his
deathbed when he turned to his wife and said, "Honey, before
I die, be totally honest with me. Is our youngest son my
child?" The wife replied, "I swear on everything that he is
your son." With that, the husband passed away. The wife
muttered, "Thank God he didn't ask about the other three."

I farted in a room full of hipsters.
They spent two hours arguing who heard it first.

Jokes for the Modern Age

Why do cows wear bells?
Because their horns don't work.

A kid was doing horribly in math class..
He always brought home an F or C- on his report card. His parents decided to put him in a private catholic school to help him improve. All of a sudden his grades improved drastically. He had an A+ on every report card for Math. His parents finally asked, "Son, what changed? How did you improve so much in your Math class?" He responded, "Well, when I walked in to class on the first day, I saw a picture of a man nailed to a plus sign, so I knew they meant business."

I dated a couple of anorexic girls once.
Two birds, one stone.

I could tell that my parents hated me.
My bath toys were a toaster and a radio.

I told my psychiatrist that I've been hearing voices.
He told me that I don't have a psychiatrist.

A farmer counted 196 cows in the field.
But when he rounded them up, he had 200.

If I had a dollar for every existential crisis I've had...
... Does money even matter?

A traveling salesman knocks on a door. A 10 year old kid answers holding a scotch and a cigar. The salesman asks,

"Are your parents home?" The kid answers, "What the fuck do you think?"

A British couple decided to adopt a German baby.
They raised him for years. However, they began to get worried, because he never spoke, and they believed that he was mentally handicapped, going as far as to take him to therapy, which was fruitless. Then, when the child was 8 years old, he had a Strudel, and said, "It is a little tepid."
His parents, of course shocked that he was suddenly speaking, asked, "Wolfgang, why have you never spoken before?", to which the child replied, "Up until now, everything had been satisfactory."

A woman and her neighbor are on her roof in Houston waiting for rescue.
While they're waiting, the neighbor notices a baseball cap floating through the flood waters. Suddenly, to her surprise, the baseball cap turns around and starts floating the other way. After going some ways, it turns around and floats back again. She observes this going on for some time, back and forth in a pattern, until she decides to point it out.
"Do you see that baseball cap? Isn't that the strangest thing you've ever seen?" "Oh, that?" replies the woman. "That's my husband. I told him he's mowing the lawn today come hell or high water."

She told me she was too classy to sleep with a married man...
Something I wish she'd mentioned before our honeymoon.

In a way, good friends are like condoms...

46

Jokes for the Modern Age

...they protect you when things get hard.

My mom didn't like my report card. I told her okay.
She said she wanted more A's.
So I told her "okaaaaay".

"I'm sorry" and "my bad" basically mean the same thing.
Except at a funeral.

A man walks into a bar, and sees King Kong having a drink.
Now, the man loves all of Kong's films, so he decides to walk
up to him. He says, "Wow! King Kong! I'm such a big fan.
Sorry to bother you, but do you have time for a photo? "
King Kong suddenly looks up, checks his watch. He turns to
the man and says, "Sorry, I've a plane to catch".

I accidentally combined Fahrenheit and milliliters...
FmL

What's the difference between a blind sniper and a
constipated owl?
One shoots, but can't hit. The other hoots, but can't shit.

I was at a disco last night.
They played the twist. I did the twist.
They played jump. So I jumped.
They played come on Eileen. I got kicked out.

A mother is helping her son study for a test : She asks him
"What is the capital of Germany?"

He replies "Berlin."
She then asks "What is the capital of France?"
He replies "Berlin."
She asks "What is the capital of Russia?"
He replies "Berlin."
She then hugs him and says "Great job Adolf, you'll do so well on your geography exam!"

Why is Kim Jong-un so evil?
He doesn't have a Seoul.

I was at the bank going to withdraw money from my account when the clerk told me I had an outstanding balance.
I told her thank you. I did gymnastics as a kid.

Algebra was always easy for the Romans..
x was always 10.

Bullies and sperm have in common::
The One-in-a-Million chance of becoming a Human Being.

I bought my son a trampoline for his birthday, and he hasn't even used it.
He just sits and cries in his wheelchair.

I can't believe my neighbor had the audacity to ring my doorbell at 2 in the morning.
Lucky for him though I was still up playing my bagpipes.

When I drink Alcohol, everybody says I'm an Alcoholic..

Jokes for the Modern Age

When I drink Fanta, nobody says I'm Fantastic.

What do a tornado and a redneck divorce have in common?
Someone is losing a trailer.

Why can't blind people go skydiving?
It scares their dogs.

A sandwich walks into a bar and asks for a drink.
The bartender says, "I'm sorry, we don't serve food here."

There's no 'I' in team...
...but there's five in 'individual brilliance'.

What is a pirate's favorite letter?
You'd think it'd be "R", but me heart belongs to the "C".

What do you get when you cross alcohol and literature?
Tequila Mockingbird

I almost witnessed a murder.
Luckily, only one crow showed up.

What's the difference between America and Yogurt?
If you leave yogurt alone for 300 years it develops a culture.

A bartender squeezes all the juice from a lemon and says, "I'll
give a thousand bucks to whoever can squeeze another drop
from this lemon." All the strongest men in the bar took turns
trying, but nobody could even squeeze a single drop. The

bartender thought he'd won, when a thin, wiry, old man walked up from the back. He grabbed the lemon, and six drops were squeezed out. Flabbergasted, the bartender asked, "How did you do that? What did you do for a living? Were you a lumberjack, or a body builder?" The old man smiled, and said, "I worked for the IRS."

Mosquito bit me 8 times.
Mosquito byte.

Grammar:
The difference between knowing your shit and knowing you're shit.

How do you end two deaf persons' arguing?
Switch off the light.

Life is like a box of chocolates.... it is destroyed remarkably fast by an emotional woman.

A guy in a plane stood up & shouted, "HIJACK!"
All passengers got scared.. From the other end of the plane a guy shouted back, "HI JOHN."

If 666 is the mark of the beast...
... and the beast is pure evil, wouldn't 25.8069758011278803 technically be the root of all evil?

What's the difference between Stephen Hawking and the computer he's hooked up to?
The computer runs.

I've changed so much since my GF told me she's pregnant.
For example my name, address and even phone number

I got pulled over a while ago and the officer asked me, "You drinking?"
I responded, "You buying?" We both laughed and I got arrested.

If you think your microwave and your TV spying on you is bad.
Your vacuum cleaner has been gathering dirt on you for years.

Did you hear about the robbers who broke into the police station and stole all the toilet seats?
It happened last week and the cops still don't have anything to go on.

How do you hide an Elephant in the jungle?
Paint his balls red and hide him in the top of a cherry tree.
Whats the loudest noise in the jungle?
A giraffe eating cherries.

A knight comes to the royal castle with a bag and asks for king's attention.
He enters, and says, "Your Majesty, I kept my word. Here's the head of the dragon!" and takes the head of the dragon out of the bag.

A royal advisor brings a bag to the king. The king replies, "Well, then, I kept my word too. Here's the hand of the princess!"

I bought my friend an elephant for their room,
They said, "Thank you"
I said, "Don't mention it"

If you ever feel lonely...just dim the lights and watch a couple of horror movies. After a while, you won't feel like you're alone anymore.

A doctor wanted to write a prescription, so he reached in his pocket and pulled out a thermometer. "Shit," he said, "some asshole has my pen."

Ever since I got Pornhub Premium local women in my area haven't been interested in me.
Help what do I do?

I'm in so much debt, I can't afford to pay my electric bill. These are the darkest days of my life.

Why doesn't the army have anyone named Will?
They were all fired at.

I was in a taxi and the driver said ,"I love my job. I'm my own boss and nobody tells me what to do!"
I said, "That's really great. Now take a left here."
It's well known that men can read maps better than women.

But that's because only men can convince themselves an inch is the same thing as 100 miles.

I poured root beer in a square glass.
Now I just have beer.

What are the two types of weather in Islamic countries?
It's either Sunni or Shi'ite

Why did the cannibal live on his own?
He was fed up with other people.

When I die
I want my last words to be, " I left a million dollars under the..."

A Scrabble game got dumped all over the interstate highway.
That's the word on the street at least.

If you're ever skydiving and your parachute doesn't deploy, you don't need to worry.
You have to rest of your life to fix it.

What do dyslexic zombies eat?
Brians

I was on a first date last night. We were at a bar, and when I looked at her, I couldn't believe how beautiful she was. I started to go weak at the knees and sweat all over my forehead.

It was only then I realized that I had drugged the wrong drink.

The statement "You are what you eat" isn't really true.
If you eat a vegetarian, you probably aren't a vegetarian.

What do you call a blonde with two brain cells?
Pregnant

Me: "When I donate blood, I do not need to extract it myself.
A nurse does it for me."
Receptionist: "Yes, but this is a sperm bank, and it doesn't
work that way!"

I recently failed out of military school when I was asked what
steps I would take to ensure my safety during a terrorist
attack.
Apparently, 'Fucking large ones' wasn't the right answer.

Two pilots are sitting in the cockpit, talking, when they
realize they are flying over a huge crater. "Wow, what a
beautiful sight," says the first pilot. "It is, isn't it?" the other
pilot replies. Then a flight attended joins them. "Sir, what are
we flying over?" she asks the first pilot. "It's a crater. A
meteor crashed into the earth and left that giant hole." "Wow,"
replies the flight attendant. "And what's that building right
next to it?" "That's the visitors center," the second pilot says.
"Phew," she says. "They really got lucky, didn't they?"

If a tree falls in the forest and no one is around to hear it...
then my illegal log cutting business is doing well.

Jokes for the Modern Age

David was a victim of ID theft
He's now known as Dav.

My local cinema was robbed last night of $754.
The thieves took a bag of maltesers, a pick n mix and a large drink.

A pirate captain tells his first mate, "Find out what be the Roman numeral for the two."
"Aye aye!" responds the first mate.

Three mice are arguing whether the holes are part of the cheese or not.
The one that thought they WERE went to the wise old owl for advice. When he got back, the cheese was gone. He asked the other two mice:
"What happened to the cheese?"
They replied:
"We decided to agree with you, so we split the cheese into thirds, and your third happened to be the holes."
Bennedict Cumberbatch just said in a press conference that he wants to do 15 years more of Sherlock!
I mean, shit, that like, 6 episodes to look forward to!

I once knew twins who were exactly alike except one was missing an eye.
They were dentical twins.

A man walks into a bar.
He was immediately disqualified from the limbo competition.

Why do the Jedi refuse to measure temperature using Kelvin?
Because only a Sith deals in absolutes.

Ever wondered why atheists don't solve exponential equations?
It's because they don't believe in higher powers.

Many people can't fall asleep due to some obsessive thoughts.
Been thinking about this all night.

I used to be addicted to hokey pokey.
But then I turned myself around.

Three men were in a boat with 4 cigarettes, but there was no
way to light them. What did they do?
Threw one cigarette overboard and the boat became a
cigarette lighter.

I asked the engineer, "What's 2+2?"
He replied, "4 ... No, 5 just to be safe."

Sherlock Holmes and Dr. Watson were going camping. They
pitched their tent under the stars and went to sleep. Sometime
in the middle of the night, Holmes woke Watson up and said,
"Watson, look up at the sky, and tell me what you see."
Watson replied, "I see millions and millions of stars." Holmes
said, "And what do you deduce from that?" Watson replied,
"Well, if there are millions and millions of stars, and if even a
few of those have planets, it's quite likely that there are some
planets like Earth out there. And if there are a few planets like

Earth out there, there might also be life." And Holmes said, "Watson, you idiot, it means somebody stole our tent."

I have 6 eyes, 3 ears, 2 mouths, but one tooth. What am I?
Ugly

The doctor gave me 6 months to live. So I killed him.
The Judge gave me 80 years. Problem solved.

What do you get when you cross a Jehovah's Witness with a Hell's Angel?
Someone who knocks on your door and tells you to fuck off.

How many software engineers does it take to change a light bulb?
None, it's a hardware problem.

My boss arrived at work in a brand-new Lamborghini.
I said, "Wow, that's an amazing car!" He replied, "If you work hard, put all your hours in, and strive for excellence, I'll get another one next year".

A man is late for work, and desperately tries to find a parking space.
His boss has already told him before that if he is late one more time, he'll be fired on the spot.
The man is circling around the parking lot, but still all the spaces are completely full.
Suddenly, the man stops his car, puts his hands together and looks towards the sky.

"Dear Almighty God!" he says, "Please let a space be free! I need this job! I promise if you give me a space, I'll quit smoking, quit drinking and only have sex again once I am married. Please God, help me out..."

Then, when the man looks down, he sees it. A free space, just ahead on his left. It shines in a golden beam of light coming down from the clouds. The man looks up once more and says, "Actually, God, it's alright. I just found a space."

I'd make a joke about unemployment.
But it doesn't work.

Did you hear the department of transportation is laying off thousands of workers?
They invented a shovel that stands up by itself.

A politician is walking down the street when he is suddenly attacked. The assailant says, "Give me all your money". The politician says, "Do you know who I am? I'm an important government official". The mugger says, "Fine, give me all my money."

STORY

A monocle walks into a bar. After a few drinks he starts to feel pretty good (and a little uncoordinated). He reaches for a cigarette, but the bartender stops him. "Sorry, buddy, but due to city ordinances we don't allow smoking in here. You'll have to step outside to smoke."

So the monocle hops off the bar stool and grabs his cigarettes to head outside. Meanwhile a second monocle emerges from the bathroom. They bump into each other as they cross paths and fall to the floor, hopelessly entangled. They try to get free, but the more they struggle, the more tangled they become.

The bartender looks down on this travesty and shakes his head. "Hey you two!" he shouts. "Stop making spectacles of yourselves!

A woman was in bed with her lover when she heard her husband opening the front door.

"Hurry!" she said, "stand in the corner." She quickly rubbed baby oil all over him and then she dusted him with talcum powder. "Don't move until I tell you to," she whispered. "Just pretend you're a statue."

"What's this, honey?" the husband inquired as he entered the room.

"Oh, it's just a statue," she replied nonchalantly. "The Smiths bought one for their bedroom. I liked it so much, I got one for us too."

No more was said about the statue, not even later that night when they went to sleep. Around two in the morning the husband got out of bed, went to the kitchen and returned a while later with a sandwich and a glass of milk.

"Here," he said to the 'statue', "eat something. I stood like an idiot at the Smiths' for three days and nobody offered me as much as a glass of water."

A woman brought a very limp duck into a veterinary surgeon. As she laid her pet on the table, the vet pulled out his stethoscope and listened to the bird's chest.

After a moment or two, the vet shook his head and sadly said, "I'm sorry, your duck, Cuddles, has passed away."

The distressed woman wailed, "Are you sure?" "Yes, I am sure. Your duck is dead," replied the vet.

"How can you be so sure?" she protested. "I mean you haven't done any testing on him or anything. He might just be in a coma or something."

The vet rolled his eyes, turned around and left the room. He returned a few minutes later with a black Labrador Retriever. As the duck's owner looked on in amazement, the dog stood on his hind legs, put his front paws on the examination table and sniffed the duck from top to bottom. He then looked up at the vet with sad eyes and shook his head.

The vet patted the dog on the head and took it out of the room. A few minutes later he returned with a cat. The cat jumped on the table and also delicately sniffed the bird from head to foot. The cat sat back on its haunches, shook its head, meowed softly and strolled out of the room.

The vet looked at the woman and said, "I'm sorry, but as I said, this is most definitely, 100% certifiably, a dead duck."

The vet turned to his computer terminal, hit a few keys and produced a bill, which he handed to the woman..

The duck's owner, still in shock, took the bill. "$150!" she cried, "$150 just to tell me my duck is dead!"

The vet shrugged, "I'm sorry. If you had just taken my word for it, the bill would have been $20, but with the Lab Report and the Cat Scan, it's now $150."

Little Johnny went to his first rodeo with his mom and dad. Dad went off to buy a beer, and little Johnny happened to spy the bull's cock flopping around beneath his belly. "Mommy, mommy! What's that long thing beneath the bull's belly!?" Johnny asks, pointing. Embarrassed, his mom looks away and mutters, "Oh, don't worry about that, Johnny. That's nothing."Dad comes back and mom goes off to use the washroom. Once mommy is gone, Little Johnny asks, "Daddy, what's that long thing beneath the bull's belly?""That's the bull's cock, son," his dad answers. "He uses it to mount and fuck a cow.""But mommy said it was nothing!" Johnny replied. Dad leans back with his hand behind his head and takes a sip of his beer. "Son... I've spoiled that woman..."

Two men are walking their dogs (a doberman and a chihuahua) when they see a restaurant.
They're pretty hungry, do they decide to head in for a bite to eat. Unfortunately, they see a sign out front that says "NO DOGS ALLOWED".
The man with the doberman says "I know what to do, just follow my lead." He throws on a pair of sunglasses and walks in.
The waiter tells him "I'm sorry sir, we don't allow dogs here."
The man says "Oh, you don't understand. I'm blind and this is my guide dog."
"A doberman for a guide dog?" The waiter asks, skeptical.
"Yes." The man replies. "Dobermans are very loyal. They're easy to train and protective too. They're born for the job."
The waiter sighs and leads the man to a table.
The second man, excited by this idea, throws on his sunglasses and walks in.
The waiter tells him "I'm sorry sir, we don't allow dogs here."
The man says "Oh, you don't understand. I'm blind and this is my guide dog."
"A chihuahua for a guide dog?" The waiter asks.
"A chihuahua?" The man asks. "They gave me a chihuahua?!"

A young boy deposit 100$ everyday in the bank. One day the general manager noticed the young boy and asked the clerk about him. He then told him that the young boy comes everyday and deposit exactly $100 each time. So the manager told the clerk to send him the little boy the next time he comes to the bank. The next day the boy comes in and he's sent to meet the manager.

The manager : "So tell me, how do you get $100 a day?"

The boy : "Well, everyday i have a bet with a different guy."

The manager : "About what?"

The boy : "About the fact that I can kiss my right eye!"

Then the manager replies : "Haha no way…"

The boy : "We can bet if you really want to…"

The manager was confident and gave his consent to the boy. A few seconds later the boy takes off his ocular prosthesis and kisses it.

The manager felt so stupid that he asked the young boy to give him back his $100. The boy agreed to give it back but under one condition.

The boy : "Let's have another bet… I'm pretty sure that you are wearing red girly panties. If I'm wrong I will give you back your $100 plus another $100 for this bet."

The manager is feeling over confident cause he knows that he isn't wearing this kind of panties and said yes.

Then the boy said again, "But before you get undressed we need to have 10 eyewitnesses to make it legit."

The manager was ok about it and called all his staff. After taking off his pants, the manager felt happy cause he just won $100, but he then notices that the young boy was so happy about losing his money that he asked him., "How can you be so happy about losing your money?"

The boy replied , "Well I had a bet with your staff about how many minutes I'll need to make you take off your pants... and guess who won?!"

A man gets on a bus, and ends up sitting next to a very attractive nun. Enamored with her, he asks if he can have sex with her. Naturally, she says no, and gets off the bus. The man goes to the bus driver and asks him if he knows of a way for him to have sex with the nun. "Well," says the bus driver, "every night at 8 o'clock, she goes to the cemetery to pray. If you dress up as God, I'm sure you could convince her to have sex with you." The man decides to try it, and dresses up in his best God costume. At eight, he sees the nun and appears before her. "Oh, God!" she exclaims. "Take me with you!" The man tells the nun that she must first have sex with him to prove her loyalty. The nun says yes, but tells him she prefers anal sex. Before you know it, they're getting down to it, having nasty, grunty, loud sex. After it's over, the man pulls off his God disguise. "Ha, ha! I'm the man from the bus!" "Ha, ha!" says the nun, removing her costume. "I'm the bus driver!"

"I want to kill my wife", says one. "Why not ask Arti, over there", says the other man, pointing to a man at the fruit-machine. "Arti over there is a top hitman," the friend goes on. So the man approaches Arti. "Are you Arti the hitman?" asks the man. "Sure am", replies Arti. "You couldn't murder my wife for me, could you?" asks the man. "I can", replies Arti, "And you know, I promised my Master, who taught me the noble art of assassination, that I would do my one hundredth kill for a fee of just one dollar, and give the client two further kills for free". "Great", says the man"could you kill my wife, her sister and my mother in law". "OK", replies Arti. "Get them to go to grocery store tomorrow at 10:00am". "Right", says the man. The following day the man's wife, her sister and his mother-in-law are tricked by the man to go to the grocery store. In walks Arti and in no time at all he strangles the wife, her sister and mother-in-law. All the newspapers lead with the same headline the following day – "ARTI CHOKES 3 FOR A DOLLAR"

I bought a Ouija board recently from a strange old man...
I got it home, laid out the pieces and before I could even ask it a question the planchette started to move around, it eventually spelled
I'VE GOT A MESSAGE TO YOU
'What is your message?' I asked.
YOU SHOULD BE DANCING
Fear started flushing over me, 'Why should I be dancing?'
NIGHT FEVER
I started to become more confused then frightened now, I needed to get to the bottom of this. 'You're talking gibberish' I shouted!
JIVE TALKIN. HOW DEEP IS YOUR LOVE. STAYING ALIVE...
'God damn it!' I shouted. That old bastard sold me a Bee Gee board!

Two old ladies were outside their nursing home, having a smoke when it started to rain. One of the ladies pulled out a condom, cut off the end, put it over her cigarette and continued smoking.

Lady 1: "What's that?"

Lady 2: "A condom. This way my cigarette doesn't get wet."

Lady 1: "Where did you get it?"

Lady 2: "You can get them at any drugstore."

The next day ... Lady 1 hobbles herself into the local drugstore and announces to the pharmacist that she wants a box of condoms. The guy looks at her kind of strangely (she is, after all, over 80 years of age), but politely asks what brand she prefers.

Lady 1: "It doesn't matter as long as it fits a Camel."

A C-130 is being escorted by two F-16s

Tired from following the slow-moving plane, one of the F-16 pilots tells his partner, "Hey watch what I can do." With that, he leaves the C-130's side and performs a series of barrel rolls. "That's nothing" says the second F-16 pilot and he also leaves his spot and does even more spectacular tricks. The two F-16s continue showing off. When they finally fall back into place the C-130 pilot comes on the mike.

"I bet I can do something you can't." he says.

"Yeah, right, prove it" says one of the F-16 pilots.

"Watch this," says the C-130 pilot and continues flying in a straight line. After a few minutes, the F-16 pilot comes back on the mic and says

"We didn't see anything, you liar" "You're the liar" the C-130 pilot says, "I went to the bathroom for a smoke break and a dump."

Late one night a drunk guy is showing some friends around his brand new apartment.

The last stop is the bedroom, where a big brass gong sits next to the bed.

"What's that gong for?" the friend asks him.

"It's not a gong," the drunk replies. "It's a talking clock."

"How does it work?"

The guy picks up a hammer, gives the gong an ear-shattering pound, and steps back. Suddenly, someone on the other side of the wall screams, "Hey asshole! It's 3:30 in the fucking morning!"

A Korean man and a Jewish man are in a bar, total strangers to one another.

The Jewish man walks up to the Korean man and, totally unprompted, punches him in the face.

Naturally, the Korean man goes "What was that for?"

The Jewish man responds, "That was for Pearl Harbor."

"Pearl Harbor? That was the Japanese," says the Korean man.

"Ah, Korean, Chinese, Japanese — you guys are all the same."

Looking not to argue, they part ways.

Later in the night, the Korean man walks up to the Jewish man, and punches him in the face as well.

"Okay, okay, I get it — that's fair. I punched you, you punched me, but what was that for?"

"That was for the titanic," says the Korean man.

"The Titanic? That was an iceberg."

"Yeah — Greenberg, Goldberg, Iceberg. You're all the same."

Jokes for the Modern Age

An Italian, a Mexican, and a Blonde American are working construction.

The three men eat lunch together each day at the top of the building they are constructing.

The Italian opens his lunchbox and exclaims "Seriously!? Spaghetti again? If my wife packs this one more time, I swear I'm jumping off this building."

The Mexican opens his too. "Tacos again? I'm with you. I'm jumping tomorrow if it happens again."

The blonde opens up his lunch box and pulls out a PB&J sandwich. "Another PB&J!" He cries. "I'm jumping tomorrow too if I get a PB&J in my lunch again."

The next day, the Italian opens his lunch, pulls out a Tupperware of spaghetti, and jumps to his death. The Mexican pulls out a bag of tacos, and immediately follows the Italian off of the building. The Blonde pulls out a PB&J, sighs, and jumps to his death as well.

A few days later at the funeral, the Italian and Mexican's wives are in tears. Both exclaim that if they had known, they would have packed something different and the men would still be alive. The women notice the wife of the Blonde, standing there and not shedding a tear.

They ask the wife of the Blonde "How can you not be upset? Your husband is dead because he kept getting the same food!" The wife of the blonde replies "Don't look at me. He packed his own lunch."

A married man was having an affair with his secretary
One day, their passions overcame them and they took off for her house, where they made passionate love all afternoon.

Exhausted from the wild sex, they fell asleep, awakening around 8pm. As the man threw on his clothes, he told the woman to take his shoes outside and rub them through the grass and dirt. Mystified, she nonetheless complied. He slipped into his shoes and drove home. "Where have you been?" demanded his wife when he entered the house. "Darling, I can't lie to you. I've been having an affair with my secretary and we've been having sex all afternoon. I fell asleep and didn't wake up until eight o'clock". The wife glanced down at his shoes and said "You lying bastard! You've been playing golf!"

An old Russian Communist is on his deathbed.
His friends are gathered around him all somber. The old man turns to one of them and says,
"Vasya, remember in 1921 you were almost executed? Well, you should know that I ratted you out to the Cheka. I hope you forgive me."
"Oh, no worries buddy." says Vasya.
The Communist then turns to another friend.
"Petya, remember being sentenced in 1937 to 25 years in the gulag? Well, it was me who went to the NKVD. Please forgive me."
"No hard feelings, my friend. You are forgiven" says Petya.
"Misha, I must confess to you that I had you sent to the penal battalion in 1942. I am terribly sorry about that day."
"Please my friend, we all forgive you. You may go in peace" says Misha.
"Thank you so much guys for being with me throughout all these years" says the old communist with a tear streaming

down his face. "I don't know where I'd be if it wasn't for you. I never knew you loved me that much despite me being a stool pigeon."

His friends are visibly touched by his words. Finally, gathers his last strength and says.

"And in honor of our deep friendship I want you to fulfill my last wish. See that cactus plant on the windowsill? As soon as I die, I want you to take it and shove it up my ass."

Just as his friends were about to say something, the old communist took his last breath and died.

So Petya rushes to the window, takes the cactus plant off and together they shove it up their dead friend's butt. Suddenly, the friends hear a loud banging on the door followed by a gruff voice shouting:

"Open up, it's the police. We've received information that an old Bolshevik has been tortured to death."

A woman in a supermarket is following a grandfather and his badly behaved 3 year-old grandson.

It's obvious to her that he has his hands full with the child screaming for sweets, biscuits, you name it. Meanwhile, Grandpa is working his way around, saying in a controlled voice, "Easy William, we won't be long . . . easy, boy."

Another outburst and she hears the grandpa calmly say, "It's okay, William, just a couple more minutes and we'll be out of here. Hang in there, boy."

At the checkout, the little terror is throwing items out of the cart and Grandpa says again in a controlled voice, "William, William, relax buddy, don't get upset. We'll be home in five minutes, stay cool, William." Very impressed, the woman goes outside where the grandfather is loading his groceries and the boy into the car.

She says to the elderly man, "It's none of my business, but you were amazing in there. I don't know how you did it. That whole time you kept your composure, and no matter how loud and disruptive he got, you just calmly kept saying 'things would be okay.' William is very lucky to have you as his grandpa."

"Thanks," said the grandpa, "but I'm William. The little shit's name is Kevin."

On a Thursday near the end of the day a teacher tells the class that whoever can name the person who said a famous quote could have Friday off.

Teacher "Ok class, who can tell me who said 'There is nothing to fear but fear itself'?

Sally excitedly shouts "FDR!"

Teacher "That's correct Sally, you can have tomorrow off."

Sally responds "No thanks. I'm Japanese and we value our education so I'll be here tomorrow."

Teacher "Ok then, let's give someone else a chance. Can anyone tell me who said 'Ask not what your country can do for you but what you can do for your country.'

Billy shouts out "JFK!"

Teacher "That right Billy, enjoy your Friday off"

Billy "No thank you, I'm a Mexican and we have a hard work ethic and I'm committed to school so I'll be here tomorrow"

Teacher "Well I guess no one wants tomorrow off. Let's continue with the next lesson"

As the teacher turns around to write on the board an angry Johnny in the back of the room mumbles "Fuckin foreigners."

The teacher snaps around and in a demanding voice asks "Who said that?"

Johnny jumps up and shouts "Donald Trump! See you losers on Monday."

Eddie wanted desperately to have sex with the hot girl at work ...but, she had a boyfriend.

One day he got so desperate he went up to her and said, "I'll pay you 100$ if you have sex with me."

The girl looked at him shocked and said, "Hell, no!'

He said, "It'll be real quick, I'll throw the money on the ground, you'll bend over to pick it up, I'll be done by the time you pick it up!"

She told him she'd have to ask her boyfriend.

So, she called him and explained the situation.

He said, "Just pick it up really fast, he won't even be able to take his pants down."

She agreed with this plan and hung up.

30 minutes go by and the boyfriend is still waiting for her call.

Finally, after 45 minutes the boyfriend called and said, "What the fuck happened?"

Breathing hard, she replied, "That bastard had all QUARTERS!"

A lawyer married a woman who had previously divorced ten husbands

On their wedding night, she told her new husband, "Please be gentle, I'm still a virgin."

"What?" said the puzzled groom. "How can that be if you've been married ten times?"

"Well, Husband #1 was a sales representative: he just kept telling me how great it was going to be.

Husband #2 was in software services: he was never really sure how it was supposed to function, but he said he'd look into it and get back to me.

Husband #3 was from field services: he said everything checked out diagnostically but he just couldn't get the system up.

Husband #4 was in telemarketing: even though he knew he had the order, he didn't know when he would be able to deliver.

Husband #5 was an engineer: he understood the basic process but wanted three years to research, implement, and design a new state-of-the-art method.

Husband #6 was from finance and administration: he thought he knew how, but he wasn't sure whether it was his job or not.

Husband #7 was in marketing: although he had a nice product, he was never sure how to position it.

Husband #8 was a psychologist: all he ever did was talk about it.

Husband #9 was a gynecologist: all he did was look at it.

Husband #10 was a stamp collector: all he ever did was lick the stamps. God! I miss him! But now that I've married you, I'm really excited!"

"Good," said the new husband, "but, why?"

"You're a lawyer. This time I know I'm gonna get screwed!"

There was a king ready to abdicate. So he brought in his 3 sons. He tells them, "Each of you will receive a trial, the first to complete their trial will become king."

Beginning with his eldest son, a brave and foolhardy man of great stature he says, "You are to bring me your grandmother's emerald ring, lost decades ago in the wreck of the Windbreaker, from the bottom of the stormy North Sea." "Right away, Father." said the eldest son, departing at once, determined to become king.

Then to his middle son, Nimble and Self-righteous, "You are to retrieve your great grandfather's shield, bearing our coat of arms, from the deadly jungles of India, lost at the site of a battle since forgotten." "I shall do so at once, Father." said the middle son, and so he too departed at once.

Then he beckoned for his youngest son, a young man Intelligent, but meek next to his older siblings, to approach. "Yes, Father?" The son inquired. To which the King replies, "Bring me a coke, I never liked those assholes."

A Texan walks into an Irish bar and clears his voice to the crowd of drinkers. He says, "I hear you Irish are a bunch of hard drinkers. I'll give $500 American dollars to anybody in here who can drink 10 pints of Guinness back-to-back."

The room is quiet and no one takes up the Texan's offer. One man even leaves. Ten minutes later the same gentleman who left shows back up and taps the Texan on the shoulder. "Is your bet still good?", asks the Irishman.

The Texan says yes and asks the bartender to line up 10 pints of Guinness. Immediately the Irishman tears into all 10 of the pint glasses drinking them all back-to-back. The other pub patrons cheer as the Texan sits in amazement.

The Texan gives the Irishman the $500 and says, "If ya don't mind me askin', where did you go for that 10 minutes you were gone?"

The Irishman replies, "Oh...I had to go to the pub down the street to see if I could do it first".

Three guys died and when they got to the pearly gates....

St. Peter met them there. St. Peter said, "I know that you guys are forgiven because you're here. Before I let you into Heaven, I have to ask you something. You have to have a car in Heaven because Heaven is so big, what kind of car you get will depend on your answer."

The first guy walks up and Peter asks the first guy, "How long were you married?"

The first guy says, "24 years." "Did you ever cheat on your wife?", Peter asked. The guy said, "Yeah, 7 times...but you said I was forgiven."

Peter said, "Yeah, but that's not too good. Here's a Pinto to drive."

The second guy walks up and gets the same question from Peter.

The second guy said, "I was married for 41 years and cheated on her once, but that was our first year and we really worked it out good."

Peter said, "I'm pleased to hear that, here's a Lincoln."

The 3rd guy walked up and said, "Peter, I know what you're going to ask. I was married for 63 years and didn't even look at another woman! I treated my wife like a queen!"

Peter said, "That's what I like to hear. Here's a Jaguar!"

A few days later, the 2 guys with the Lincoln and the Pinto saw the guy with the Jaguar crying on the golden sidewalk. When they asked the guy with the Jaguar what was wrong, he said, "I just saw my wife, she was on a skateboard!"

A guy walks into a bar with his monkey.

While at the bar, the monkey won't stop jumping from here and there, messing with the fridge, with the tables, until a moment that he ate a pool ball.

The bartender said to the monkey's owner, "Did you see what your monkey did? He ate a pool ball."

The guy said "I'm sorry, the monkey is a troublemaker. I'll pay for it, don't worry."

So, he pays the bill and the ball and goes away.

Another day, he comes back with his monkey again. The monkey, as done before, started jumping through the whole bar until a moment that he stopped near an olive plate. He picked one olive, shove it at his ass, took it back and ate it.

The bartender said, "Hey, did you see what your monkey did? He put an olive in the ass then ate it."

The guy said, "Well, after that pool ball, he learned to measure everything before eating."

A balding, white haired man walked into a jewelry store this past Friday evening with a beautiful much younger gal at his side. He told the jeweler he was looking for a special ring for his girlfriend. The jeweler looked through his stock and brought out a $5,000 ring.

The man said, "No, I'd like to see something more special."

At that statement, the jeweler went to his special stock and brought another ring over. "Here's a stunning ring at only $40,000" the jeweler said.

The lady's eyes sparkled and her whole body trembled with excitement.

The old man seeing this said, "We'll take it."

The jeweler asked how payment would be made and the man stated,

"By check. I know you need to make sure my check is good, so I'll write it now and you can call the bank Monday to verify the funds. I'll pick the ring up Monday afternoon."

On Monday morning, the jeweler angrily phoned the old man and said "Sir... there's no money in that account."

"I know," said the old man... "But let me tell you about my weekend."

A tired American soldier is on a train to London. The train was packed. He went searching for a seat as he came by a middle aged woman and her dog. He asked her "may I please have that seat", the woman replied "you Americans are so rude, cant you see my little Fifi is sitting here". The soldier walks the length of the train and back to cross the woman and her dog again. He asks again "may I please have that seat". The woman replies again "not only are you Americans rude but also arrogant". The man picked up the dog and threw him out the train window. The woman screamed and yelped for help and justice as a man from the other side of the cart yelled, "It's true you Americans do everything wrong. You eat with the wrong fork, you drive on the wrong side of the road, and now you threw the wrong bitch out of the window".

There's an Air Force guy driving from Wagga to Richmond, and an Army guy driving from Richmond to Wagga. In the middle of the night with no other cars on the road they hit each other head on and both cars go flying off in different directions. The Air Force guy manages to climb out of his car and surveys the damage. He looks at his twisted car and says,"Man, I am really lucky to be alive!"

Likewise the Army guy scrambles out of his car and looks at his wreckage. He too says to himself, "I can't believe I survived this wreck!"

The Army guy walks over to the Air Force guy and says, "Hey man, I think this is a sign from God that we should put away our petty differences and live as friends instead of arch rivals"

The Air Force guy thinks for a moment and says, "You know, you're absolutely right! We should be friends. Now I'm gonna see what else survived this wreck"

So the Air Force guy pops open his boot and finds a full, unopened bottle of Jack Daniels.

He says to the Army guy, "I think this is another sign from God that we should toast to our new found understanding and friendship"

The Army guy replies, "You're damn right!" and he grabs the bottle and starts sucking down Jack Daniels. After putting away nearly half the bottle the Army guy hands it back to the Air Force guy and says, "Your turn!"

The Air Force guy twists the cap back on the bottle and says, "Nahh, I think I'll wait for the cops to show up."

I once spent a month in the slammer.

It wasn't that bad. The guards were friendly. My cell-mate was a cool guy. The food was better than my wife's. I didn't see any fights. I wasn't assaulted or raped.

On my last day a guard walked me out to the exit gate. We chatted about football on the way. As the gate opened he said to me, "Goodbye and good luck. How do you feel?"

"I feel good, man," I replied. "I'm happy to finally be out."

Then he smacked me hard across the skull with his baton, drawing blood. I was like, "What the hell, dude?"

"That's for ending your sentence with a preposition."

The year is 2024 and the new POTUS has been elected. The newly sworn-in president is sitting at the desk in the oval office tending to some paperwork. The doors open and in walk a few secret service agents.

"Excuse us Mr. President, but we were looking over some of the documents about your background and noticed that your physical health and performance records are outdated. We ask that you come with us to perform some tests."

The president agrees, gets up out of his chair and follows the group of agents to a private and secluded athletics field.

"This won't take long Mr. President, simple tests. First off, we need you to do as many push-ups as you can without stopping." and so the president gets down, takes a deep breath and does a strong 62 push-ups.

"Good job sir, next we need you to hold these weights out in front of you and do as many squats as you can without stopping"

The president gets in his best stance and begins squatting. He does a burly 45 squats before giving out.

"Impressive sir, just one more test. We need you to run a mile around this track as fast as you can."

The president tightens the laces on his shoes, adjusts his headband and takes a quick drink of water, then gets on the starting line. The agents count him off and he takes off running. Several minutes later he passes through the finish line sweating and breathing hard.

"Very good sir, that's one of the most impressive mile lap times I've ever seen."

The president says "Am I the best?'

The agent takes a second to flip through some papers on his clipboard before going "Ehh.. not quite. You're second best overall with a time of 10 minutes and 32 seconds."

The president says, "What? Who did better than me?"

"Well, Bush did 9:11."

A man rushes into a bar and orders a double brandy. While the barman is pouring, the man extends his hand at knee height and asks: "Do penguins grow this big?"

"I should think so," the barman replies.

The man raises his hand. "How about this big?"

"Well, perhaps a king penguin, but I'm not sure . . ."

The man holds his hand at shoulder level: "This big?"

"Not a cat in hell's chance."

The man knocks back his drink in one. "Hell. I just ran over a nun."

A man walks into a bar and orders three beers.

The bartender brings him the three beers, and the man proceeds to alternately sip one, then the other, then the third, until they're gone.

He then orders three more and the bartender says, "Sir, I know you like them cold, so you can start with one, and I'll bring you a fresh one as soon as you're low."

The man says, "You don't understand. I have two brothers, one in Australia and one in the Ireland. We made a vow to each other that every Saturday night, we'd still drink together. So right now, my brothers have three beers, too, and we're drinking together."

The bartender thinks it's a wonderful tradition, and every week he sets up the guy's three beers. Then one week, the man comes in and orders only two. He drinks them and then orders two more. The bartender says sadly, "Knowing your tradition, I'd just like to just say that I'm sorry you've lost a brother."

The man replies, "Oh, my brothers are fine -- I just quit drinking."

NASA was interviewing professionals to be sent to Mars. Only one could go and couldn't return to Earth The first applicant, an engineer, was asked how much he wanted to be paid for going. "A million dollars," he answered, "because I want to donate it to M.I.T."

The next applicant, a doctor, was asked the same question. He asked for $2 million. "I want to give a million to my family," he explained, "and leave the other million for the advancement of medical research."

The last applicant was a lawyer. When asked how much money he wanted, he whispered in the interviewer's ear, "Three million dollars."

"Why so much more than the others?" asked the interviewer.

The lawyer replied, "If you give me $3 million, I'll give you $1 million, I'll keep $1 million, and we'll send the engineer to Mars."

A teacher is teaching her class of kindergartners how to use grown-up expressions.

She points to little Sally and asks, "Sally, what did you do this weekend."

Sally tilted her head and said, "I went on a choo choo!"

"Marvelous, dear," said the teacher, "But next time, try 'I rode on a train.'"

She then turns to little Mark, a kindly, young lad and asks, "And how about you, Mark?"

Mark put a finger to his lips and thought real hard. "I went to the animal place and saw the stripy horsies."

"Simply exquisite," the teacher replied, "But say you saw zebras at the zoo next time, alright dear?"

After Mark nodded, the teacher turned to colorful and spirited Franky. "How about you, Frank?"

The little boy tilted his head after a second and said, "I read a...book!"

"Very good!" The teacher said, glowing with pride. "And what did you read?" She asked, beaming.

Frank thought long and hard for a second, then smiled real big, puffed up his chest and said in a great, big voice:

"Winnie the Shit!"

Little Eddy has really upset the girls at school.

After months of enduring his foul language and sexual innuendos in class, the girls one day get together before class and decide, if today, Eddy says anything even remotely sexual or offensive, we will all get up at the same time and walk out in protest.

Class starts and the teacher says, "OK kids, today's subject will be buildings and construction. Who can tell me how buildings are made?"

The class remains quiet, then little Eddy raises his hand and says, "Madam, I know."

The teacher says, "OK Eddy, please explain."

Eddy says, "Well, first before anything you need a permit from the city for the construction project to begin, that could take months. Once you get the permit, then come the bulldozers to basically dig into the earth to create the foundation. Then, cement is poured into the foundation and pylons are inserted. Around the pylons, the outer structure of the building is made, floors, walls, ceilings. Then comes wiring and plumbing. Next drywall can be installed along with flooring and fixtures. When all is said and done, you still have to get an occupancy permit from the city before you can actually use the building."

The class remains quiet.

The teacher says, "WOW Eddy! Bravo, that was amazing, how did you learn all that?"

Eddy says, "For the past many months, just a few doors down from our house, they have been building what I think is a huge whore house, I've watched the whole thing from start to finish."

At that moment, all the girls suddenly get up and start to walk out.

Eddy looks around and says, "Whoa whoa whoa, girls sit down, they are not hiring yet, still waiting for final permit."

A beautiful blonde woman ends up sitting next to a professor on a plane. He's amused by her ditsy attitude, and the two start playing a trivia game. The blonde agrees to pay a dollar for every question she gets wrong, and the professor, feeling pompous, offers to pay a hundred dollars for his incorrect answers.

After missing the first question, the blonde asks something along the lines of, "What goes up a hill wet, then comes down the hill dry?" The professor spends the whole ride trying to solve the riddle, but eventually gives up and hands the blonde a hundred dollar bill when the plane lands.

As she stands up to leave, the professor asks, "So what does go up a hill wet, then down a hill dry?" ...at which point the blonde takes out another dollar and hands it to him with a wink.

A Muslim dies and goes to heaven

He is about to climb up the white clouded stairs and stops in front of a golden gate. There is a bearded man waiting for him. The Muslim asks: "Are you Mohammed?" "No, I'm St. Peter. Mohammed is higher up" The Muslim is very happy to hear that Mohammed is more important than Saint Peter and is higher up. He climbs another flight of stairs. Tired, he stops in front of another large gate. He finds a young man with curly blond hairs and asks: "Are you Mohammed?" "No, I'm Michael, Mohammed is higher up."The Muslim is in ecstasy learning that Mohammed is more important than angels. He climbs an even longer flight of stairs. Exhausted, he reaches another, even bigger gate. He is met by a bearded man and asks him, "Are you Mohammed?" "No. I am Jesus. Mohammed is further up" The Muslim is ecstatic and explodes with happiness learning that Mohammed is even more important than Jesus and that his religion is indeed the best of them all. He cannot wait to meet Mohammed. He quickly climbs further up. Panting, breathless, exhausted, he arrives at a huge white gate. Waiting for him is very old man with a long white beard. The Muslim asks with the little breath he has left, "Are you Mohammed?" "No. I'm God, but I see you're tired, come in, seat down, rest for a moment. Do you want some water, a coffee perhaps? And the Muslim says: "Yes, a coffee ... I would be very grateful." So God turns around, raises his hand, whistles, and says. "Mohammed, two coffees."

Counting CONDOMS
A boy goes to the drug store with his dad and sees the condom display.

Boy: "Dad, why do they do packs of one condom?"

Dad: "Those are for the high-schoolers for Friday nights."

Boy: "So, why do they make packs of three?"

Dad: "For the college guys for Friday, Saturday and Sunday nights."

Boy: "Then why do they make packs of 12?"

Dad: "Those are for married couples -- you know, January, February, March."

God said "Adam, I want you to do something for me"

Adam said, "Gladly, Lord, what do You want me to do ?"

God said, "Go down into that valley"

Adam said, "What's a valley ?"

God explained it to him. Then God said,

"Cross the River."

Adam said, "What's a river ?"

God explained that to him, and then said,

"Go over to the hill…"

Adam said, "What is a hill?"

So, God explained to Adam what a hill was

He told Adam, "On the other side of the hill you will find a cave"

Adam said, "What's a cave?"

After God explained, He said, "In the cave you will find a woman"

Adam said, "What's a woman?" So God explained that to him, too

Then, God said, "I want you to reproduce"

Adam said, "How do I do that?"

God first said (under His breath), "Geez …"

And then, just like everything else, God explained that to Adam as well.

So, Adam goes down into the valley, across the river, and over the hill, into the cave, and finds the woman

In about five minutes, he was back

God, His patience wearing thin, said angrily,

"What is it?"

Adam said, "What's a Headache?"

A woman in a hot air balloon realized she was lost...

A woman in a hot air balloon realized she was lost. She reduced altitude and spotted a man below. She descended a bit more and shouted: "'Excuse me, can you help me? I promised a friend I would meet him an hour ago but I don't know where I am".

The man below replied "You're in a hot air balloon hovering approximately 30 feet above the ground. You're between 40 and 41 degrees north latitude and between 59 and 60 degrees west longitude". "You must be a technician." said the balloonist. "I am" replied the man "how did you know?" "Well," answered the balloonist, "everything you have told me is probably technically correct, but I've no idea what to make of your information and the fact is, I'm still lost. Frankly, you've not been much help at all. If anything, you've delayed my trip with your talk."

The man below responded, "You must be in management." "I am", replied the balloonist, "but how did you know?" "Well," said the man, "you don't know where you are or where you're going. You have risen to where you are, due to a large quantity of hot air. You made a promise, which you've no idea how to keep, and you expect people beneath you to solve your problems. The fact is you are in exactly the same position you were in before we met, but now, somehow, it's my fucking fault!"

A little boy comes home from school and tells his father, "I got an F in math today." His father replies, "What happened?" The boy says, "Well, my teacher asked me, 'What's 3 times 2', and I said 6.'" The father replies, "Well, that's correct." The boy says, "I know. Then she asked me, 'What's 2 times 3.'"

The father then replies, "What the fuck is the difference?" The boys says, "That's what I said!"

The next day the little boy comes home from school and tells his father, "I got an F in PE today." His father replies, "What happened?" The boy says, "Well, my teacher asked me to raise both my hands, and I did." The father replies, "And?" The boy says, "Then he asked me to raise my left leg and I did. Next he asked my to raise my right leg!" The father then replies, "How the fuck were you supposed to stand? On your cock?" The boys says, "That's what I said!"

The following day the boy comes and tells his dad principal wants to see his parents. His father replies, "What happened this time?" The boy says, "Well, they said they wanted to see me in the principal's office and when I went there, there were the principal, my math teacher, the PE teacher, and the art teacher. The father then replies, "What the fuck was the art teacher doing there?" The boys says, "That's what I said!"

A young New York woman was so depressed she decided to end her life by throwing herself into the ocean.

Just before she could throw herself from the docks, a handsome young man stopped her. "You have so much to live for," he said. "I'm a sailor and we are off to Italy tomorrow. I can stow you away on my ship. I'll take care of you, bring you food every day, and keep you happy. When we get to Italy you will be SO GLAD you're alive"

With nothing to lose and always wanting to see Italy, she accepted.

That night, the sailor brought her aboard and hid her in a small but comfortable compartment in the ship's hold.

From then on, every night, he would bring her sandwiches, a bottle of red wine, and make love to her until dawn.

Two weeks later she was discovered by the captain during a routine inspection.

"What are you doing here?" asked the captain.

"I have an arrangement with a sailor," she replied. "He brings me food and I get a free trip to Italy."

"I see," The captain says.

Then her conscience got the best of her, and she added, "Plus, he's screwing me."

"He certainly is," replied the captain. "This is the Staten Island Ferry."

A nurse got a new job at a new hospital. Her boss thought that she knew everything about the job, except for ONE THING: "Never laugh at a patient, no matter what."

"Of course I won't laugh," the nurse said. "I'm a professional nurse. In over twenty years I've never laughed at a patient."

Three days later, the hospital received a new patient that the nurse was in charge of. "I have a problem with my sexual organs," the man said. "Okay, just drop your trousers for me," the nurse responded.

"Okay then," Fred said, and proceeded to drop his trousers, revealing the tiniest penis the nurse had ever seen. Length and width, it couldn't have been bigger than an AAA battery.

Unable to control herself, the nurse started giggling then almost fell to the floor laughing. A few minutes later she was able to regain her composure. "I'm so sorry," said the nurse. "I don't know what came over me. On my honor as a nurse and a lady, I promise it won't happen again. Now tell me, what seems to be the problem?"

"It's swollen," Fred replied.

A farmer walks into the bar and sits down beside me looking extremely agitated.

"What's goin' on with ya Pete?"

"Ah jesus, Brian. So I got up early and was milking my biggest cow in her stall. I had a pail just about full when she kicked her right leg and spilled the entire thing."

"Aw Christ, Pete. I'm sorry about that."

"So, pissed off, I found a length of rope and tied her right leg to her stall so she wouldn't kick again and went back to milking her. I had this second pail just over half full when CRASH her left leg jolts and knocks it all over the floor. I'm fuming so I went and found another length of rope and tied her left leg to her stall nice and tight and propped the pail up again. No way to kick it over now, right?"

"Aye,"

"Well about a quarter full, her tail whips around the handle of the bucket and sends it flying. So I go stomping around looking for another length of rope but couldn't find anything. I thought, ah, this bitch deserves the belt anyways. So I took off the belt holding up my pants and tied her tail to the crossbeam above her stall."

"Don't tell me she kicked it over again."

"Nah, then my wife walked in.

"God bless Mommy, Daddy and Grammy. Goodbye Grampa."

One evening a father overheard his son saying his prayers "God bless Mommy, Daddy and Grammy. Goodbye Grampa."

Well, the father thought it was strange, but he soon forgot about it.

The next day, the Grandfather died.

A month later the father heard his son saying prayers again: "God bless Mommy. God bless Daddy. Goodbye Grammy."

The next day the grandmother died.

Well, the father was getting more than a little worried about the whole situation.

One week later, the father once again overheard his sons prayers. "God Bless Mommy. Good bye Daddy."

This nearly gave the father a heart attack.

He didn't say anything but he got up early to go to work, so that he would miss the traffic.

He stayed all through lunch and dinner.

Finally after midnight he went home.

He was still alive!

When he got home he apologized to his wife.

"I am sorry Honey. I had a very bad day at work today."

"You think you've had a bad day? YOU THINK YOU'VE HAD A BAD DAY!?" the wife yelled, "The mailman dropped dead on my doorstep this morning!"

Two men are sitting in the cinema waiting for the movie to start

so they get bored with all the commercials and suddenly one of the two notices a bald guy in the middle of the front row. So he tells his friend " 5 bucks if i go smash his head ? ". The other guy curious about the outcome likes the idea so he agrees. The man stands up goes down the stairs smashes the bald guy on the head and says to him " Hey Mike , long time no see man " . The bald guy clearly surprised responds "I believe you made a mistake sir" so the guy replies " I'm so so sorry sir " and walks away. The two friends laugh and the man gives the 5 bucks to his rather bold friend. After 5 minutes the guy tells his friend again "10 bucks if I do it again ? " the friend agrees and so the man goes and smashes the bald guy's head again and says "Hey mike how have you been man ? " . The bald guy now clearly irritated tells him " Hey man listen , I've already told you I'm not Mike " and the guy responds " A thousand apologies sir , won't happen again" and goes back to his friend who is now dying of laughter while the bald guy in the front row switches seats and sits now in the corner. After receiving his money he tells his friend again " 50 bucks if i do it one last time ? " so his friend who is dying of curiosity agrees. Once again the man goes down and to the bald guy who is now sitting in the corner and smashes his head while shouting " Oh come on Mike , you've been sitting here all along and I've been smashing that pour guy's head for 15 minutes ? "

A doctor was having an affair with his nurse. Shortly afterward, she told him she was pregnant. Not wanting his wife to know, he gave the nurse a sum of money and asked her to go to Italy and have the baby there.
"But how will I let you know the baby is born?" she asked.
He replied, "Just send me a postcard and write 'spaghetti' on the back.
I'll take care of expenses."

Not knowing what else to do, the nurse took the money and flew to Italy.

Six months went by and then one day the doctor's wife called him at the office and explained, "Dear, you received a very strange postcard in the mail today from Europe, and I don't understand what it means."

The doctor said, "Just wait until I get home and I will explain it to you."

Later that evening, the doctor came home, read the postcard, fell to the floor with a heart attack. Paramedics rushed him to the ER.

The lead medic stayed back to comfort the wife.

He asked what trauma had precipitated the cardiac arrest.

So the wife picked up the card and read, "'Spaghetti, Spaghetti, Spaghetti, Spaghetti - Two with sausage and meatballs, two without.'"

A lawyer is pulled over by a cop

The officer asks the lawyer, "Do you know why I pulled you over?"

"I haven't the foggiest idea," said the lawyer.

The officer replied, "You didn't make a full stop at the stop sign back there. You only slowed down."

The lawyer thinks for a few seconds then says, "If you can prove to me the difference between stopping and slowing down, I'll take full responsibility. Otherwise, you let me off with a warning. Sound fair?"

The officer ponders it shortly before nodding his head. "Sounds fair. Can you step out of the car please?"

Just as the lawyer steps out and shuts the car door, the officer pulls out his baton and starts beating the lawyer. After a few swings, the officer says, "Now, would you like me to stop or slow down?"

A man walks into a bar with his pet alligator.

Bar man: "You need to leave because if that alligator bites someone I'll get sued!"

Alligator owner: "No no he's tame! Watch I'll prove it."

He then zips down his fly and puts his cock inside the alligators mouth. The alligator keeps its mouth open the whole time. He then zips his pants back up and says, "See I told you he was tame! Anyone else like to try?"

Drunk guy at the bar: "Yeah Id like to try but I don't think I can keep my mouth open that long."

Once a man was traveling through the west on vacation, when he saw a sign that said, "Meet the Indian Who Never Forgets, Next Exit". Well, being curious, the man stops at the attraction to see the Indian. He asks the man, "What did you have for breakfast on June 9, 1978?" The Indian replies "Eggs!"

Well, everyone has eggs for breakfast, this guy is a charlatan, the man thinks.

10 years later, the same man is on vacation again, and sees the sign for the Indian again. He thinks what the heck, I'll stop in and see him.

When the man approaches the Indian, he holds up his hand and says, "How!"

The Indian replies, "Scrambled."

A guy is working at a grocery store and a lady comes up to him and asks: "Hello young man, can you tell me where the broccoli is?" "Oh I'm sorry madam, we ran out of broccoli, we will have some tomorrow." "Oh okay," says the lady and the guy goes back to his work. Then somebody taps him on his shoulder, he turns around and there's the same lady and she goes: "Sir, i can't find any broccoli." "We are fresh out of broccoli ma'am, we will have some tomorrow." and he goes back to work. And then the woman comes right in front of him and says very loudly: "Where the hell is the broccoli?" And he says: "Madam, how do you spell cat? As is catastrophic." "C-A-T" "Good, good ... and how do you spell dog? As in dogmatic." "D-O-G" "Great, great ... and how do you spell fuck? As in broccoli." "There is no fuck in broccoli." "AND THAT'S WHAT I'M TRYING TO TELL YOU!!!"

A man walked out to the street and caught a taxi just going by. He got into the taxi and the cabbie said, "Perfect timing. You're just like Brian."
Passenger: "Who?"
Cabbie: "Brian Sullivan. He's a guy who did everything right all the time. Like my coming along when you needed a cab, things happen like that to Brian every single time."
Passenger: "There are always a few clouds over everybody."
Cabbie: "Not Brian. He was a terrific athlete. He could have won the Grand Slam at tennis. He could golf with the pros. He sang like an opera baritone and danced like a Broadway star and you should have heard him play the piano. He was an amazing guy."

Passenger: "Sounds like he was something really special."

Cabbie: "There's more. He had a memory like a computer. He remembered everybody's birthday. He knew all about wine, which foods to order and which fork to eat them with. He could fix anything. Not like me. I change a fuse and the whole street blacks out. But Brian, he could do everything right."

Passenger: "Wow. Some guy then."

Cabbie: "He always knew the quickest way to go in traffic and avoid traffic jams. Not like me, I always seem to get stuck in them. But Brian, he never made a mistake and he really knew how to treat a woman and make her feel good. He would never answer her back even if she was in the wrong; and his clothing was always immaculate, shoes polished too. He was the perfect man! He never made a mistake. No one could ever measure up to Brian Sullivan."

Passenger: "An amazing fellow. How did you meet him?"

Cabbie: "Well, I never actually met Brian. He died. I'm married to his bloody widow."

A wife was making breakfast for her husband when he ran into the kitchen with an alarmed expression

"TURN 'EM EGGS!! TURN'EM BEFORE THEY BURN!!!".

"GOOD LORD, WE ARE GOING TO NEED MORE BUTTER!!! GET IT! GET IT!!! DAMN THEY ARE GOING TO STICK!!!"

The wife looked at him with a puzzled expression and continued.

"HOLY SHIT! NOT SO MUCH SALT AND PEPPER!!! JUST A BIT!! YOU WILL RUIN THEM!!!"

The wife turned around and shouted, "WHAT THE FUCK IS WRONG WITH YOU?!"

"Nothing", replied the husband in a calm and even tone. "Just wanted to give you an idea of what it's like when I am driving with you by my side."

So there's this guy, and he's got an ant farm, but not like a normal ant farm. It's like a regular farm that's run by ants, and one day the ant in charge of the farmer ants says to the guy, "Hey guy, we're workin' our thoraxes off tryin' to harvest these crops but it's real tough, boss. See they're all the way up in the trees and we're super small. I think we need some bigger ants to help us get the job done." So the guy's like, "Shit, I guess i did notice that production's been pretty minimal. I guess I could try to get you some bigger ants. Aren't most of you pretty much all the same size though?" And the ant's all, "Yo that's racist." So they guy's like, "Whoa whoa whoa. I didn't mean it like that, just relatively in size to a tree. Look I'll go right now to get us some taller ants to help your team." So the guy goes to the unemployment center in town and asks around for some tall ants, but they've all been hired by other farms that can offer health insurance. He tried to recruit some practice squad players in the ant basketball league but couldn't match their salaries. He even tried to convince an ant warden to give him his tallest ants in a prisoner work release program but the warden wanted a percentage of everything sold, and one of the tall ant inmates spit on the guy while he was there. So he decided that wouldn't work either. He was walking down the street tired, frustrated, and desperate, when he came across a super tall homeless ant holding a "WILL WORK FOR FOOD" sign. So the guy is really excited, thinking he's found his solution and explains to the hobo ant that his farmer ants aren't tall enough, and the homeless ant starts laughing in his face. "Maaaaan you don't need bigger ants, you need smaller trees!" said the ant. The guy was shocked at how simple and elegant the hobo ant's solution was, but also furious that he'd spent an entire day looking for tall ants. He decided he needed a drink to ease his mind so he stopped in the nearest bar. So the guy goes to the bartender, "Hey, barkeep. Lemme get 4 shots of the strongest booze you got." And the bartender's like, "Brother, I've got some moonshine that'll melt your face off, but it's crazy strong. You sure you want 4 shots?" And the guy says, "Look man, I've had a nightmare of a day. I know my limits. Trust me, I can handle my shit." So the bartender's like, "Alright man if you insist." And he lines up four shots of the moonshine, and the guy wastes no time and throws em back, one after another, slams down the fourth shot glass, and then immediately projectile vomits all over the bar, including on the bartender. The bartender's fuckin piiiiiissed and yells, "What the fuck man!? You said you could handle your shit!! What is your problem!?!?" And the guy wipes his mouth and says, "Duuuuude, sorry. I thought I hadda hire taller ants."

Little Joe: "Daddy, how much does my wiener weigh?"
Dad: "I don't know, I guess about 3 ounces"
Little Joe: "And how much does your wiener weigh?"
Dad: "I don't know, I guess about 15 ounces?"
Little Joe is intrigued and goes to his grandfather.
Little Joe: "Granddad, how much does your wiener weigh?"

Granddad: "I don't know, but it must be a lot, because your grandmother can't get it up"

A elderly couple by the names of George and Martha go to church one Sunday. Unfortunately, Martha has a terrible habit of falling asleep during the service, and it embarrassed George something awful. So the sly old man came up with a plan. Every time his wife would nod off, he'd prick her with a needle.

So the sermon starts and the preacher works up the crowd with a couple "hallelujahs" and "amens," and sure enough, old Martha nods off.

George readies the pin and, just as the priest says, "And to whom, my faithful servants, do we owe everything good in our lives?" George gives his wife a sharp jab in the side, to which she responds with a powerful, "My God!"

The preacher basks in the enthusiasm of his disciples and continues on with the sermon as though nothing has happened.

Martha, embarrassed and confused, rubs her side and continues on worshiping. George slips the pin out of sight, pleased by the results.

Not fifteen minutes later, as the preacher whips his worshipers into another frenzy of praise and passion, old Martha starts nodding off. Her eyelids are drooping and her head's beginning to tilt.

George, always quick to take notice, readies his secret weapon again, poising it just off his wife's hip. Sure enough, just as the preacher calls to the crowd, "And who, my beloved warriors of light, died for our sins?" he jabs it home.

Martha jolts as if she's been electrified and gasps loudly amid the others, "Jesus Christ!"

The preacher takes their word as gospel and continues.

George quickly slips the pin under his leg once more, looking innocent as a newborn.

Martha, with her side smarting, falls back into a pattern of fervent worship.

Not twenty minutes later, however, the poor old girl is beginning to nod off yet again. George, in his sly state, takes note immediately, and readies the pin for yet another assault.

Just as the preacher shouts to the heavens, "Now, my children, what did Eve say to Adam after siring their 99th child?" George makes one final jab, but this time Martha sees it, and she shouts:

"IF YOU STICK THAT THING IN ME ONE MORE TIME, YOU OLD BASTARD, I'LL BREAK IT IN HALF AND SHOVE IT UP YOUR ASS SIDEWAYS!"

One day, Einstein has to go to an important science conference.

On the way there, he tells his driver that looks a bit like him: "I'm sick of all these conferences. I always say the same things over and over!"

The driver agrees. "You're right. As your driver, I attended all of them, and even though I don't know anything about science, I could give the conference in your place."

"That's a great idea!" says Einstein. "Let's switch places then!"

So they switch clothes and as soon as they arrive, the driver dressed as Einstein goes on stage and starts giving the usual speech, while the real Einstein, dressed as the car driver, attends it.

But in the crowd, there is one scientist who wants to impress everyone and thinks of a very difficult question to ask Einstein, hoping he won't be able to respond. So this guy stands up and interrupts the conference by posing his very difficult question. The whole room goes silent, holding their breath, waiting for the response.

The driver looks at him, dead in the eye, and says, "Sir, your question is so easy to answer that I'm going to let my driver reply to it for me."

Three friends are fishing when a crocodile comes ashore and grants them three wishes..

The first friend says, "I wish I could catch a huge marlin."

The crocodile swims away for a moment, then comes back. The friend then pulls in a massive marlin.

"Amazing!" Says the second friend "Well you know what? I wish I were rich."

The crocodile then swims underwater and fetches a treasure chest full of money and gold and gives it to him.

"INCREDIBLE!" says the third friend "I've got a better one, I wish my penis touched the ground!"

The crocodile bites his legs off.

A woman was at a gas station filling her car with gas. She inserted the nozzle and began filling the car with gas. As she waited for the car to fill, she lit a cigarette and began to smoke it. The filler clicked to indicate it was full of gas, and she pulled the filler out of the car. Some gas leaked out of the filler onto her sweater arm, and a spark from the cigarette lit her arm on fire. The woman began to scream for help, and waved her arm about trying to put the fire out. A highway patrolman who happened to be nearby ran over and saw the woman flailing about in pain. Without hesitation, he pulled his handgun out of the holster and shot her three times.

A few weeks later in court, the judge asked the patrolman why on earth he shot that woman?

The patrolman answers, "Well your honor, she was waving around a firearm!"

There once was a guy named Juan. He was a really nice guy....didn't beat his wife, didn't beat his kids, didn't beat the aardvark in the backyard. He lived in a small country in South America. Juan lived a simple life, and was simply happy.

One day, he was sitting in a coffee shop with a few friends, when the topic of the election for mayor came up. One of his friends said, "Hey, Juan. Why don't you run? You're a really great guy!" Juan smiled and thanked his friends for their kindness, but they were persistent, as they should be...he was a great candidate and a great guy; he didn't beat his wife, or his kids, or the aardvark in the backyard. Juan reluctantly agreed, and posted a few signs out to announce his candidacy; he thought of it as kinda a joke. Well, as it turned out, when word got around that Juan was running, his popularity grew fast. 'Wow, Juan is running?' 'What a great guy!' 'I heard he doesn't beat his wife, or his kids!' 'Yeah, nor the aardvark in the backyard!' Well, to nobodies surprise (except Juan), he won by a landslide (the other candidate was Oliver North), and was sworn into office with a very surprised look on his face. Well, he saw that there was do getting out of it, so he decided to do his best.

And his best was quite good. The town prospered like it never had before. The crime for the year consisted of someone dropping a lollipop stick on the sidewalk. He spent 6% of the budget, and donated the rest to the Dum Fiters Relief Fund. The townspeople were ecstatic, and his performance turned a lot of heads. Everyone in the town was thrilled with Juan as mayor; he didn't beat his wife, or his kids, or the aardvark in the backyard. Well, at the end of the year, with his term almost up, Juan was pretty pooped. As he sat in the coffee shop with his friends, reflecting on the year, one suggested that, despite the town's success, the province was in some financial trouble. 'Heck, with Juan's record, he should be governor!' another smiled. Juan wondered why everyone's eyes lit up suddenly. Within hours the campaign was on. All the ads and posters had the same theme: 'Vote for Juan! He doesn't beat his wife, or his kids, or the aardvark in the backyard!' When election day came, there was no doubt about the winner; Juan had been in the lead since the week he had entered. Governor Juan sat back in his padded chair and went to work once again.

His record was brilliant for the two years he spent as governor. The crime rate fell by 2/3, the budget was balanced, education rose sharply, and the province's Soccer Team sold out every game that Juan attended (he was a big Soccer Buff). The whole country was now buzzing with Juan;s work. Everyone commented how he was such a great guy, how he didn't beat his wife, how he didn't beat his kids, and how he didn't beat the aardvark in the backyard. Then the President was shot. This meant that they needed a new president. Normally, they would turn to the vice-president, except for the fact in this case was that the vice-president was the murderer. Hmm. The Governors got together to decide on a new President for the remaining three years of the term. Each one walked into the room with a mail sack full of letters, all of which has similar messages: 'Juan for President!' 'Let Juan preside as President!' 'How can you not select Juan? He doesn't beat his wife, doesn't beat his kids, and doesn't beat the aardvark in the backyard? What else do you want?' To make a very long story not quite as long, Juan was quickly named president, and the country was glad he did. The country prospered; new trade agreements were made, old disputes were settled, and there was peace throughout the country. Juan was a national hero. One day Juan came home from work exhausted. He put his briefcase down and plopped down in his easy chair. His mind was racing, but he was exhausted. He couldn't concentrate...pressure from everyone...lobbyists want this...governors want that....everyone wants this and that and acccccckkkkk!!!!!! Juan looked out the window into the backyard. As usual, the aardvark was out there slurping up ants. Wander....wander....sluuuurp! Wander.....wander....sluuuurp! The monotonous repetition snapped something in Juan's mind. A sudden rage built up inside of him, something evil and uncontrollable. He stood. Unfortunately for Juan, his neighbor heard the cracks and quickly moved the telescope from Juan's upstairs window, where his daughter was undressing, down to the yard, and witnessed the brutal attack. He immediately phoned the police, and within hours, Juan was behind bars, the aardvark rushed to the hospital, and the telescope back up to the upstairs window. The country was horrified, and the citizens called for nothing less than the usual penalty given out for this type of crime....death by firing squad. It was granted, and the punishment was to be carried out swiftly. Juan stood there, broken and insane.

The firing squad levied their guns at him. 'Ready.......'
'Aim.........' Suddenly, and without warning, the aardvark leaped from the shadows, aimed at Juan and fired a golf gun. The shot boomed throughout the town, and the shot itself went clear through Juan's heart and out his back.

You may be asking yourself in between sobs what a golf gun is? This, in itself, is the morale of the story....

The answer...well, I don't know. But it sure made a hole-in-Juan

A psychologist has a party for all of her patients. She instructs everyone to come dressed as an emotion. As the party begins, she sees her first patient come in dressed in all red. The psychologist asks her "what are you dressed as" and the patient replies, "I'm dressed as anger and rage." The next patient comes in and is dressed in all blue. The psychologist ask what he is dressed as and he tells her, "I'm dressed as sorrow." Next patient comes in dressed in yellow. The psychologist says, "What are you dressed as?" She responds, "I'm dressed as happiness and delight." Then she sees her black patient Leroy come into the party, completely naked with a pear on the end of his dick. The psychologist goes up to him and says, "Leroy, you are at my party completely naked with a pear on your penis. What on earth are you doing?" And Leroy says, "What do you mean what am I doing? You told me to come to this party dressed as an emotion and I am." The psychologist in disbelieve says,

"What emotion could you possibly be???" He tells her, "I'm deeply in dis pear."

A 34 year-old man had undergone plastic surgery to make himself look like a 20 year old. He wanted to test and see if other people could guess his correct age. He went to a nearby shop and asked the shop keeper to guess what age he was.

The shop keeper replied, "About 20 years old".

The man was overjoyed that the surgery had made him look young and walked off happily.

He went to McDonald's to get lunch afterwards and feeling confident, he asked the worker at the counter to guess what age he was.

The worker replied, "About 20 years old".

The man smiled happily. The worker asked if the answer was correct.

The man replied, "I'm actually 34 years-old".

The worker was amazed as he did not look a day over 21. The man went to a bus stop afterwards to board the bus and go home. He saw an old lady waiting for the bus. He decided to test it out on her. He asked her to guess what age he was.

The old lady said, "I know an old technique to guess people's age. If you let me caress your balls for 5 minutes I will be able to guess your age".

The man was confused but seeing as there was no one else at the bus stop he let her do it.

After 5 minutes the old lady pulls her hand out of the man's trousers and says, "You are 34 years-old".

Amazed the man asked how did she know.

The old lady replied, "I was behind you at McDonald's."

A homeless man enters a diner. He asks the waitress, "What can a guy get for a dime?" "Not much, how about a glass of water?" says the waitress. "Sure, that will do." The homeless man sits at the counter and starts drinking his water. He notices a cowboy sitting a couple seats down the counter with a big bowl of chili. The homeless man continues to drink his water. All the while the bowl remains uneaten. Finally the homeless man asks the cowboy, "Are you going to eat that chili?" "Nope, it's yours if you want it." says the cowboy. The homeless man takes the bowl and begins eating. When he gets to the bottom of the bowl, he finds a dead mouse. The homeless man immediately throws up back into the bowl. The cowboy looks at him and says, "Yep, same thing happened to me."

In a certain tribe, in which polygamy was practiced, a married man's standing in the tribe depended upon the combined weight of his wives-the greater the combined weight, the more important was the man. Every year, on weighing day, and according to custom, the married men would stand their wives on neatly spread animal skins. Then the chief of the tribe would come around with a crude seesaw and balance the wives of one man against those of another, in order to determine the relative importance of the men. Now Gog had only one wife, who was very heavy, while Gug had two much slenderer wives, and all year the two men argued as to who was the more important. When weighing day arrived, Gog placed his wife on a large hippopotamus skin, and Gug placed his wives on two small gazelle skins.

When the weighing was performed, it was found that Gog's wife exactly balanced against the two wives of Gug. Thus, it turned out that the two men were equally important, since, by the chief's ruling, "the squaw on the hippopotamus is equal to the sum of the squaws on the other two hides."

A man was just waking up from anesthesia after surgery, and his wife was sitting by his side.
His eyes fluttered open and he said, "You're beautiful." Then he fell asleep again.
His wife had never heard him say that, so she stayed by his side. After a short nap, his eyes fluttered open and he said, "You're cute!"
The wife was disappointed. She asked her husband's doctor, "When my husband first woke up, he called me beautiful, but just a minute ago, he woke up again and called me cute. What happened to 'beautiful'?" The doctor replied, "The drugs are wearing off."

In science class, 3 worms were places into 3 different jars.
The first worm was put into a jar of alcohol.
The second worm was put into a jar of cigarette smoke.
The third worm was put into a jar of soil.
After one day, these were the results:
The first worm in alcohol ---dead.
The second worm in cigarette smoke --- dead.
The 3rd worm in soil --- alive.!!
So the science teacher asked the class --- "What can you learn from this experiment.?"

Jokes for the Modern Age

A kid quickly raised his hand and said, "As long as you drink alcohol and smoke , you won't have worms in your stomach".

A woman walks into a bank in New York City and says she's going to Europe for 2 weeks, and needs to borrow $5,000. The bank clerk says they'll need some kind of collateral, and she hands them the keys to a brand-new Rolls-Royce parked in front of the bank. The bank's president and others enjoy a good laugh at the woman for using a $250,000 Rolls-Royce as collateral for a $5,000 loan. A bank employee then drives the Rolls into the bank's underground garage.
Two weeks later, the woman returns, repays the $5,000 and the interest, which is $25.41. The loan officer says "Miss, we are happy to have your business, but we're a little puzzled. We checked you out, and you're a multi-millionaire. Why would you bother to borrow $5,000?" The woman replies, "Where else in New York City can I park my car for two weeks for only $25.41 and expect it to be there when I return?"

Earl and Peggy had been married 50 years. Every year they'd attend the county fair and every year Earl would look at Peggy and say, "Look at those planes! I'd love to ride one of those planes." And every year Peggy would reply, "Yea, but it costs $10, and $10 is $10!"
Finally, the year came of Earl's 75th birthday. They go to the fair and again, Earl exclaims "Look at those planes! I'd love to ride one of those planes." To which Peggy again replied, "Yea, but $10 is $10."
The pilot overheard the exchange and chimed in, "Listen, I'll give you both a ride, and if you don't say a word or scream

during the entire ride, the ride is free. But if you do, you will owe me $20 for the ride."

Earl got so excited about his opportunity and both he and Peggy hopped on the plane. The pilot pulled out all the tricks. Barrel roles, loops, corkscrews, everything he could to get some kind of noise, but they were quiet the whole ride.

Finally they landed and the pilot said, "I can't believe you two didn't make a sound!"

Earl said to the pilot, "I was going to say something when Peggy fell out, but $10 is $10."

The FBI had an opening for an assassin. After all the background checks, interviews and testing were done, there were 3 finalists. For the final test, the FBI agents took one of the men to a large metal door and handed him a gun. "We must know that you will follow your instructions no matter what the circumstances. Inside the room you will find your wife sitting in a chair . . . Kill her!!" The man said, "You can't be serious. I could never shoot my wife." The agent said, "Then you're not the right man for this job. Take your wife and go home." The second man was given the same instructions. He took the gun and went into the room. All was quiet for about 5 minutes. The man came out with tears in his eyes, "I tried, but I can't kill my wife." The agent said, "You don't have what it takes. Take your wife home." Finally, the last man was given the same instructions, to kill his wife. He took the gun and went into the room. Shots were heard, one after another. They heard screaming, crashing, banging on the walls. After a few minutes, all was quiet. The door opened slowly and there stood the man, wiping the sweat from his brow. "Some idiot loaded the gun with blanks." he said. "I had to strangle the bitch to death."

Little Johnny went to visit his grandfather's farm for a holiday. While grandfather was showing him around the farm, he saw a cock doing his business with one of the hens, and he asked, "Grandpa, what's that?"

Grandpa replied, "That's a cock, and that's a hen, and he's serving her."

Further on, Johnny saw a horse doing his business with a mare, and he asked, "Grandpa, what's that?"

Grandpa replied, "That's a horse, and that's a mare, and he's serving her."

At dinner that night, Grandma said, "Grandpa, will you please serve the turkey?" At that, little Johnny jumped up and said, "If he does that, I'm having a hamburger!"

A dumb guy visits a hunting club and asks a hunter how he killed his first buck.

The hunter says he got his gun, went into the woods, followed the tracks, and shot the buck. The dumb guy, satisfied with the answer, soon leaves.

The following day the dumb guy returns to the hunter and asks how he shot his first rabbit. The hunter says he got his gun, went into the woods, followed the tracks, and shot the rabbit. The dumb guy leaves the hunting club.

The following day the dumb guy returns to the hunter and, still curious, asks how he shot his first bear. The hunter says he got his gun, went into the woods, followed the tracks, and shot the bear. The dumb guy leaves looking energetic and inspired!

Weeks passed without any sight of the dumb guy and the hunter, worried about his dumb friend, decides to look into it. He finds that the dumb guy is being held at the local hospital in intensive care so the hunter goes to visit.

The hunter enters the hospital room and sees the dumb guy in what seems to be a full body cast, with machines everywhere to help him breathe, eat, and ultimately stay alive. Surprised, he asked the dumb guy what happened!

The dumb guy musters all his strength to lift his head toward the hunter and in small gasps he tells the hunter his story.

"I got my gun..." "I went into the woods..." "I followed the tracks..." "And was hit by a train."

A mother is helping her son study for a test : She asks him "What is the capital of Germany?"

He replies "Berlin."

She then asks "What is the capital of France?"

He replies "Berlin."

She asks "What is the capital of Russia?"

He replies "Berlin."

She then hugs him and says "Great job Adolf, you'll do so well on your geography exam!"

A Blonde, a brunette and a redhead are trying to get to heaven. St. Peter is at the bottom of a staircase, welcoming them. "Welcome, these are the steps that lead to the gates of heaven. There are a hundred steps and at each one, I will tell an offensive joke and if you laugh, you have no business getting into heaven."

So they start their journey and it goes well for quite some time until at step 24 the redhead burst out laughing. St. Peter tells her she is not allowed to go into heaven, so she leaves.

At step 47 the brunette couldn't keep a straight face anymore, so St. Peter tells her off as well.

But the blonde is still going strong until finally, at step 99 she couldn't keep it in anymore. St. Peter looks confused

"Why are you laughing? I didn't even get to the last joke?" He said.

The blonde replied; "I just got the first joke"

Four friends reunited at a party after 30 years. After a few laughs and drinks, one of them had to go to the rest room The ones who stayed behind began to talk about their kids and their successes.

The first guy says, "I am very proud of my son, he is my pride and joy. He started working at a very successful company at the bottom of the barrel. He studied Economics, Business Administration, and was promoted, began to climb the corporate ladder, becoming the General Manager, and now he is the president of the company. He became so rich that he gave his best friend a top of the line Mercedes Benz for his birthday."

The second guy says, "Damn, that's terrific! My son is also my pride and joy, I am very proud of him. He started working at a traveling agency for a very big airline. He went to flight school to become a pilot and managed to become a partner in the company where he now owns the majority of the assets.

He became so rich that he gave his best friend a brand new jet for his birthday."

The third guy says, "Well, well, well congratulations! My son is also my pride and joy and he is also very rich. He studied in the best universities and became an Engineer. He started his own construction company and became very successful and a multimillionaire. He also gave away some very nice and expensive thing to his best friend for his birthday. He built a 30,000 sq. ft. mansion especially for his friend."

The three friends congratulated each other mutually for the successes of their sons. The fourth friend who earlier had gone to rest room returned and asked, "What's going on, what are all the congratulations for?" One of the three said, "We were talking about the pride we feel for the successes of our sons. What about your son?"

The fourth man replied, "My son is Gay and he makes a living dancing as a stripper at a nightclub."

The three friends said, "What a shame that must be, that is horrible, what a disappointment you must feel."

The fourth man replied, "No, I am not ashamed. Not at all. He is my son and I love him just as well, he is my pride and joy. In addition, he is very lucky too. His birthday just passed the other day and he received a beautiful 30,000 sq. ft. mansion, a brand new jet, and a top of the line Mercedes Benz from his three boyfriends!"

The Ice Cream Truck pulls away from Acacia Drive, having served the happiest bunch of kids all day. The driver whistles a gay tune, the sun is shining, the traffic is good, there's but a solitary car at the red light ahead. Suddenly, there's a banging on the side of the truck. Startled, he pulls away, thinking its a

114

jacking. His heart racing he makes it to the next set of lights. He turns on the radio and "Welcome To The Jungle" is playing, so he turns it up loud and starts singing, adrenaline coursing through his veins. He lets out a relieving bellow of laughter. Just before the lights change, the banging on the side happens again. He jumps up, wishing he'd carried today. He breathes in and raises the shutter, ready for whatever is awaiting him. Before him, a young woman is panting, hands on her knees, struggling for breath, sweat pouring off her brow. She'd clearly been running, strenuously.

"Well, wtf do you want, lady?", Giovanni says.

"I'm...I'm...", she gasps.

"You're what?!", he says, impatient and angry.

"...I'm vegan!", she says.

A blond and a redhead are talking one afternoon.

Redhead - "So how was your weekend?"

Blond - "Not to good my cat got it's tail cut off by the lawn mower."

Redhead - "That's terrible! What did you do about it?"

Blond - "Well I got the cat and it's tail and took it to Walmart."

Redhead - "Why wouldn't you take the cat to the vet?"

Blond - "Well I heard that Walmart was the larger retailer in the country."

A horse walks into a bar and says to the barman, "Five whiskeys please!" before downing the whole lot.

The barman looks at the horse and says, "That's quite a stomach you've got, are you an alcoholic?"

The horse says, "I don't think I am". Suddenly the horse poofs out of existence.

See the joke is a reference to Descartes the philosopher who coined the phrase "I think. Therefore I am." However explaining this prior to the joke would be putting Descartes before the horse.

A guy walks into a bar. He sits down by the bar and orders a beer. He looks around and sees a big bowl full of money. In the corner of the bar stands a medical screen. He finds all that very unusual so he asks the bartender what's it all about. The bartender replies, "You see that screen over there? Behind the screen is a very serious horse. If you put a 20 in the jar and make the horse laugh, then the money is yours." The guy thanks the bartender, finishes the beer, puts the 20 in the jar and goes behind the screen. After not even 30sec there's a deafening neighing laughter coming from behind the screen. The guy comes out, empties the jar in his bag, and leaves the bar.

2 weeks later same guy walks into the same bar, from behind the screen he can still hear laughter. He looks at the bar and again sees the jar full of money. So he sits down, orders a beer, and asks the bartender what's up.

The bartender replies, "Well, since you've left last time the horse wouldn't stop laughing. So now we decided that whoever makes him stop takes the money. Of course the usual 20 entry."

The guy acknowledged the explanation, finished his beer and went behind the screen. After maybe a minute, a huge wailing neigh raptures the entire establishment. It is agonizing.

The guy comes out, empties the jar and turns for the door.

"Hey, hold on!" shouts the bartender. "First of all, how did you make him laugh?" asks the bartender. "Simple" answers the guy, "I told him my dick is bigger than his."
"Fair enough", says the bartender, "But how the hell did you make him cry?" The guy looks the bartender in the eyes "I showed him!"

A DEA officer stopped at our farm yesterday, he said "I need to inspect your farm for illegal growing drugs."
I said "Okay, but don't go in that field over there."
The DEA officer verbally exploded saying, "Mister, I have the authority of the Federal Government with me!" Reaching into his rear pants pocket, the arrogant officer removed his badge and shoved it in my face. "See this badge?! This badge means I am allowed to go wherever I wish…. On any land !! No questions asked or answers given!! Have I made myself clear?…. do you understand?!!"
I nodded politely, apologized, and went about my chores. A short time later, I heard loud screams, looked up, and saw the DEA officer running for his life, being chased by my big old mean bull…. With every step the bull was gaining ground on the officer, and it seemed likely that he'd sure enough get gored before he reached safety. The officer was clearly terrified.
I threw down my tools, ran to the fence and yelled at the top of my lungs, "Your badge, show him your BADGE!!"

A concerned husband went to a doctor to talk about his wife
He says to the doctor, "Doctor, I think my wife is deaf because she never hears me the first time and always asks me to repeat things." "Well," the doctor replied, "go home and

tonight stand about 15 feet from her and say something to her. If she doesn't reply move about 5 feet close and say it again. Keep doing this so that we'll get an idea about the severity of her deafness".

Sure enough, the husband goes home and does exactly as instructed. He starts off about 15 feet from his wife in the kitchen as she is chopping some vegetables and says, "Honey, what's for dinner?" He hears no response.

He moves about 5 feet closer and asks again. No reply. He moves 5 feet closer. Still no reply. He gets fed up and moves right behind her, about an inch away, and asks again, "Honey, what's for dinner?"

She replies, "For the fourth time, vegetable stew!"

A man was stranded on deserted island for 10 years. One day a beautiful girl swims to shore in a wet suit.

Man: "Hi! Am I ever happy to see you!"

Girl: "Hi! It seems like you've been here along time. How long has it been since you've had a cigarette?"

Man: "It's been ten years!" With this information the girl unzips a slot on the arm of her wet suit and gives the man cigarette.

Man: "Oh, thank you so much!"

Girl: "So tell me how long it's been since you had a drink?"

Man: "It's been ten years" The girl unzips a little longer zipper on her wet suit and comes out with a flask of whiskey and gives the man a drink.

Man: "Oh, thank you so much. You are like a miracle"!

Finally the girl starts to unzip the front of her wet suit and asks the man leadingly, "So tell me then, how long has it been since you played around??"

The man looked at her and said excitedly: "Oh, my God, don't tell me you've got a set of golf clubs in there too?!?!"

The whole town is in trouble!!

A boy called up his mom from hospital, "Mom, I took tests and they declared that I have AIDS."

Mom: "What? Don't come back home son, go away."

Boy: "Why mom, I'm your son."

Mom: "You foolish boy! If you come back home, then your wife will be infected, from your wife to your brother, from your brother to our maid, from our maid to your dad, from your dad to my sister, from my sister to her husband, from her husband to me, from me to our gardener, from our gardener to your sister…

And if your sister got it, then the whole town is in trouble.

A blonde woman kept getting told she was dumb because she was blonde. She decided to dye her hair black and show people how smart she was. She approached a farmer with a herd of sheep and asked him.

-"Sir, if i can guess how many sheep you have there, will you give me one?"

-"Well ma'am, i suppose, if you guess the exact number I'll let you have one".

-"Alright, you have 134 sheep".

-"I'll be damned, that's exactly right, well, pick the one you like".

-"THIS ONE!"-"If i guess the natural color of your hair, can i have my dog back?

Two men had a tee time, and were about to get started when a man approached them, said he was alone and asked if he could join them. The two men agreed.

Making small talk, the subject of their professions came up. After the first two described their boring desk jobs, the third man said, "I'm a killer for hire. I'm one of the best in the business, I charge $10,000 a shot."

The first two men looked incredulous, so the third man reached into his golf bag, and produced a sniper rifle, and watched the mens' jaws drop. "This thing has incredible range, I can aim from miles away."

One of the men asked, "Wow, my house is pretty close by, I wonder if I can see it from here." The assassin hands him the gun, and he holds it up in the direction of his house. His lip curls and his face turns red as he witnesses through the scope his wife in their bedroom with his next-door neighbor.

"I can't believe that cheating whore and my double crossing bastard neighbor"

"Well... I am an assassin..."

"Alright, I want you to shoot my neighbor in the dick, since he couldn't keep it in his pants, and I want you shoot my wife in her stupid lying mouth." The assassin agrees, takes back his gun and lines up the shot. He waits... and waits... and waits...

"What the hell is taking you so long!?!? you said you were good at this."

"Give me a second, I'm about to save you $10,000 dollars."

A mouse and a bear find a genie lamp in the woods. The bear rubs it and a genie pops out and says, "Thank you for freeing me, for doing so I grant you both three wishes each."

The bear went first and said, "I wish the entire earth was covered in forests," and the genie makes the whole earth covered in forests.

The mouse went next and said, "I wish I had a mouse sized motorcycle," and the genie spawned him one.

The bear then wished a second time and exclaimed, "I wish the forest was filled with bears," and the genie did just that.

The mouse then told the genie, "I wish for a mouse sized motorcycle helmet," and the genie put one on his head.

For the bears final wish, he said, "I wish all the bears in the forest, except me, were female," and the genie turned all the bears in the forest except for the one who wished it female.

The mouse then got on his motorcycle, started it, and before he sped off yelled at the genie, "I WISH THE BEAR WAS GAY!"

A man is walking over a bridge and he sees a beautiful woman about to jump...

He tries to talk her down, but she's too distraught. Finally, he says to her, "Well, if you're gonna kill yourself anyway, why not give me a nice blowjob first?"

She replies, "Well, it doesn't matter anyway. I guess I might as well make somebody happy before I die."

So she climbs down off the railing and give the dude one of the most amazing experiences of his life. When it's over, he's completely dazed. "That was incredible!" he says. "Why the hell is someone as gorgeous as you with such... talents trying to kill themselves anyway?"

"It's my father. He disowned me."

"But why!?"

"For dressing up as a woman."

A cowboy named Bud was overseeing his herd in a remote mountainous pasture in Montana when suddenly a brand-new BMW advanced toward him out of a cloud of dust. The driver, a young man in a Brioni® suit, Gucci® shoes, RayBan® sunglasses and YSL® tie, leaned out the window and asked the cowboy, "If I tell you exactly how many cows and calves you have in your herd, will you give me a calf?"

Bud looks at the man, who obviously is a yuppie, then looks at his peacefully grazing herd and calmly answers, "Sure, why not?"

The yuppie parks his car, whips out his Dell® notebook computer, connects it to his Apple i phone, and surfs to a NASA page on the Internet, where he calls up a GPS satellite to get an exact fix on his location which he then feeds to another NASA satellite that scans the area in an ultra-high-resolution photo.

The young man then opens the digital photo in Adobe Photoshop® and exports it to an image processing facility in Hamburg, Germany.

Within seconds, he receives an email on his Apple iPad® that the image has been processed and the data stored. He then accesses an MS-SQL® database through an ODBC connected Excel® spreadsheet with email on his Galaxy S5® and, after a few minutes, receives a response.

Finally, he prints out a full-color, 150-page report on his hi-tech, miniaturized HP LaserJet® printer, turns to the cowboy and says, "You have exactly 1,586 cows and calves."

"That's right. Well, I guess you can take one of my calves," says Bud.

He watches the young man select one of the animals and looks on with amusement as the young man stuffs it into the trunk of his car.

Then Bud says to the young man, "Hey, if I can tell you exactly what your business is, will you give me back my calf?"

The young man thinks about it for a second and then says, "Okay, why not?"

"You're a Congressman for the U.S. Government", says Bud.

"Wow! That's correct," says the yuppie, "but how did you guess that?"

"No guessing required." answered the cowboy. "You showed up here even though nobody called you; you want to get paid for an answer I already knew, to a question I never asked. You used millions of dollars' worth of equipment trying to show me how much smarter than me you are; and you don't know sh*t about how working people make a living - or about cows, for that matter. This is a herd of sheep."

"Now give me back my dog."

Three women die in an accident together and go to heaven. They meet god at the door, and he says, "There is only one rule in heaven. Don't step on the turtles."

So they go in, and sure enough there are millions and millions of turtles on the ground, and it is near impossible not to step on one.

So the first woman accidentally steps on a turtle. Saint Peter comes and chains her hand together with the hand of the ugliest man she had seen in her life.

Later, the second woman stepped on a turtle, and Saint Peter came and chained her hand to another ugly, ugly man's hand.

The last woman was very, very careful though. She didn't step on a turtle for months. So when the 3rd month finished without her stepping on a turtle, Saint Peter came and chained her hand to a beautiful, handsome, muscular man's hand.

She says, "Do you know why we were chained up?" He replies, "I don't know about you, but I stepped on a turtle."

RELATIONSHIPS

Sometimes I hide my girlfriend's inhaler.
So the neighbors think I'm a stud when they hear her panting, "Give it to me!"

My wife packed my bags and kicked me out of the house. As I walked out the front door, she screamed, "I wish you a slow and painful death, you bastard!" "Oh," I replied, "So now you want me to stay!"

Dating is a lot like fishing...
Sure there is plenty of fish in the sea, but until I catch one, I am just stuck here holding my rod.

My girlfriend dumped me today saying I was too childish.
But today is opposite day so it's all good.

My wife left me because she thinks I'm too insecure.
No wait, she's back. She just went to make a cup of tea.

I sent my wife a picture of my flaccid penis.
Just to let her know I was thinking of her.

My girlfriend and I were having sex the other day when she looked at me and said, "Make love to me like in the movies." So I fucked her in the ass, pulled out, and came all over her face and hair. I guess we don't watch the same movies.

My wife just said to me, "Look at this, I've had this since we got married 20 years ago and it still fits me." I said, "It's a fucking scarf."

Wife: You're shirtless?
Me: Yes
Wife: And also covered in...oil?
Me: Well, you know how you always say I never glisten?
Wife: Listen! you never listen.
Me: Ohhh

My girlfriend says I'm an idiot who can't do anything right. So I packed her bags and left.

My girlfriend looked at me with her sexy eyes and said, "I want you to make me scream with your two fingers baby."....so I poked her in the eyes.

[Introducing girlfriend to my family]
Me : This is my girlfriend Janine
Janine : Hi
Wife : What the fuck

My wife found out I was cheating after she found the letters I was hiding.

She got mad and said she's never playing Scrabble with me again.

My girlfriend and I planned to commit suicide together.
But once she killed herself, things started looking a lot more positive.

I tried to re-marry my ex-wife.
But she figured out I was only after my money.

My wife was wondering why she was so itchy.
I asked why she pronounced it with a silent "B".

I could tell my wife was cheating on me when she said she was out with her friend.
Her friend has been in bed with me for the past hour. That lying, cheating bitch.
My girlfriend thinks I'm cheating on her, and I'm getting tired of it.
She sounds just like my wife.

I don't always beat my girlfriend, but when I do...
it's to the door to open it for her.

My marriage was a like a hurricane.
At the beginning there was a lot of blowing, but in the end I lost my house.

Your dog loves you more than your wife does.

Jokes for the Modern Age

Want proof? Lock them both in the trunk of your car. Let them out an hour later and see which one is happy to see you.

A wife is a sex object...
Every time you ask for sex, she objects.

My wife asked if I thought she should get a breast augmentation. I said I love her body just the way it is. She asked if I ever wished she had been born with big tits. I said nah, babies with big tits freak me out.

A wife gets naked and asks her husband, 'What turns you on more! my pretty face or my sexy body?' Husband looks her up and down for a moment and replies, 'Your sense of humor.'

Wives are like grenades.
Remove the ring and boom, the house is gone.

It's impossible to please women.
Even at your wedding, you are not the best man.

Girlfriend said that she slept with 61 men before.
I doubt it, but she insisted that I was her sixty-second man.

Husband: "I'm getting you diamonds for our anniversary." -
Wife: "Nothing would please me more."
Husband: Gets her nothing instead.

My girlfriend told me I'm bad in bed.
I told her she should learn to enjoy the little things in life.

Why are married women heavier than single women?
Single women come home, see what's in the fridge and go to bed. Married women come home, see what's in the bed and go to the fridge.

Wife has strange ways of starting a conversation...out of nowhere she'll ask me, "Are you even listening at all?"

Why are most hurricanes named after women?
When they come in, it's exciting and wet, but after they leave, half your shit's gone.

I bought a trash compactor for my ex-wife.
Or, as Victoria Secret calls it - a corset.

My wife asked me what I thought the sexiest thing was about her.
Apparently, "how much you look like your sister" was not the correct answer.

My marriage counselor asked if it was true that I generally wake up grumpy in the morning.
I said, "Nah, most of the time I just let her sleep."

I bought my wife a beautiful diamond ring for her birthday
A friend of mine said, "I thought she wanted one of those pretty 4-wheel drive vehicles?"
"She did," I replied, "But where in the world was I going to find a fake jeep!"

Pedro was sexually a very experienced man when he got married to Maria, but she was totally naive.

On their wedding night, when Pedro removed his clothes, Maria asked, 'Pedro! What is that?'

Pedro, a quick thinker, said, 'Maria, I am the only man in the world with one of these.'

And then he proudly proceeded to demonstrate to her what it was for. Maria was pleased. After their honeymoon was over, Pedro returned to work. On returning home in the evening after his first day at work post honeymoon, Pedro found a very upset Maria waiting on their front porch.

'Pedro, you said you were the only man in the world with one of those and yet today, when I saw Gonzalez changing his clothes behind the shed, he had one, too!'

Ever a fast thinker on his feet, Pedro said, 'Oh, Maria, Gonzalez is my best friend. Since I had two, I gave him one. So he is the only other man in the world with one.'

A skeptical Maria accepted this answer, but when Pedro returned home from work the following evening, an agitated Maria was waiting on the porch.

'Maria? Now what's wrong???'

'Damn it, Pedro! You gave the better one to Gonzalez!'

My girlfriend said to me the other day, "If anything ever happens to me, I want you to meet someone new." Apparently, getting stuck in traffic doesn't count as "anything".

Women call me ugly until they find out how much money I make.
Then they call me poor and ugly.

A wife says to her husband, "You're always pushing me around and talking behind my back." He says, "What do you expect? You're in a wheelchair."

My wife walked in on me while watching porn. In a panic reflex, I instantly changed to a random channel, the fishing channel. As my wife walks out again she says, "You should stay on the porn channel.. you already know how to fish."

PUNS

Caveman and a bear walk into a bar. Bartender says "what's your story?" Caveman says...
Bear with me..

I like jokes. But jokes about air conditioners?
Not a fan.

One of my friends told me that ever since they changed genders, their kids won't even look at them anymore..
It's almost as if they have become trans-parent.

What should happen to the person who invented Knock Knock jokes?
They should get a No-Bell prize.

If you have a bee in your hand, what do you have in your eye?
Beauty. Because beauty is in the eye of the bee-holder.

I'm addicted to seaweed.
I must seek kelp.

I slapped Dwayne Johnson's ass
I guess I've hit Rock Bottom.

When does a joke become a dad joke?
When the punchline becomes apparent.

I have a T-Rex who sells me guns.
He's a small arms dealer.

Why did the mermaid rush out of her maths exam, red faced
and embarrassed?
Because her algaebra didn't hold up.

Why is the letter "C" afraid of the rest of the alphabet?
Because all the other letters are Not-Cs.

My wife gets upset when I steal her kitchen utensils...
But it's a whisk I'm willing to take.

This girl said she would go out with me if I knew a six letter
word that's a synonym for "calm".
I said, "It's sedate."

What's the difference between Bill Cosby and a small fencing
sword?
One's a little rapier.

Imagine if instead of periods, women had apostrophes.
They'd be even more possessive.

I jokingly told my friend I was collecting the corpses of past
emperors of Russia and dumping them into a giant ravine.
But he thought I was serious and asked what was wrong with
me.
I guess he just doesn't understand tsar chasm.

I'm definitely the loser if I run over a deer. It's going to cost me hundreds of dollars. (needs work)
But nature is only out a buck.

How do you cut Rome in Half?
Use a pair of Caesars.

I dreamed I had drowned in an ocean made of orange soda.
When I woke, I realized it was just a Fanta sea.

A man noted for telling puns was locked into a dark closet, and told he would not be released until he made up a pun about the situation. He immediately shouted,
"Oh, pun the door"

This girl was handing out vegan pamphlets when she said she recognized me
I said I never met herbivore

Teacher : "Use dandelion in a sentence."
Jamaican student: "De cheetah is faster dandelion."

A length of rope walks into a bar
The bartender looks at him and says, "Get out, we don't serve ropes in here!"
The rope goes outside and cuts himself in half and ties his two sections together. Not pleased with his appearance, he takes a comb and combs out his ends.
He walks back into the bar and the bartender says, "Hey, aren't you that rope I just kicked out?"

And the rope replied, "No, I'm a frayed knot."

I tried to change my password to Beefstew1.
But they said it wasn't stroganoff.

Two morons are sitting on a fence. The big one fell off. Why didn't the other?
He was a little more on.

The year 2020 is going to be filled with so many puns about perfect vision.
I can just see it now.

I failed my final exam on Greek mythology.
It's always been my Achilles elbow.

What do lawyers wear to court?
Lawsuits.

Iron Man is technically a Female.

My boyfriend and I both drive a Honda.
He's got one of those boxy ones, and mine is a mid-size sedan.
And neither of us has our own place, so we mostly end up just having sex inside the car. His is a little bigger, so we usually use his.
Recently, however, he's been wanting to experiment a little bit.
And he's saying we should try some things out while having sex on top of his car, instead of inside it.

But if I'm gonna have sex with my boyfriend in a way that's out of his Element, it will have to be on my own Accord.

I'm a magician of sorts. I steal candy bars using sleight of hand.
You could say I have a few Twix up my sleeve.

What do you call a knight encircled in enemies?
Sir Rounded

Can a joke about dinosaurs make you laugh?
You bet jurassic can.

My pregnant wife asked me if I ever worried it would be too hot for the baby inside her.
I said, "Nah, it's probably womb temperature."

Why was Pavlov's hair so soft?
Classical conditioning.

A man died due to his obsession of taking photos of himself next to a boiling kettle.
He had serious selfie steam issues.

what is a Will?
It's a dead give away.

What do you call an army of babies?
An infantry.

So a guy walks into a bar and sees three steaks taped to the ceiling. He then asks the bartender, "Why are there three steaks taped to the ceiling?" The bartender says, "Well, you get one shot. If you jump up and touch one of the steaks, then you get free drinks for the rest of the day. However, if you miss, you must buy everyone else's drinks for the next hour." The guy ponders for a minute and then says, "I would do it, but the stakes are too high."

I was fired from the keyboard factory today.
I wasn't putting in enough shifts.

What washes up on small beaches?
Microwaves.

Why does a chicken coop have 2 doors?
Because if it had 4 doors, it'd be a Chicken Sedan..

What do you call a bee that lives in America?
A USB.

Why do cows have hooves?
Because they lactose.

A guy was admitted to hospital with 8 plastic horses in his stomach.
His condition is now stable.

My mum didn't think I'd give our daughter a silly name... but I called her Bluff.

My neighbor blamed my gravel for making him fall.
But it was his dumb asphalt.

I went cow tipping in a marijuana field.
The steaks were high.

I like to stand in the corner at parties and blow on anyone who walks by.
People hate it, but I'm a fan.

I tell dad jokes, but I have no kids.
I'm a faux pa.

I have a rare condition where I'm compelled to eat clay.
I've been shitting bricks all week.

Why is Kim Jong-un so evil?
He doesn't have a Seoul.

How much RAM does a great white shark have?
A killer-bite.

I have a friend who says that he hates all comforters.
I told him that he shouldn't make blanket statements like that.

I opened a company selling land mines disguised as prayer mats.

Jokes for the Modern Age

Prophets are going through the roof.

Why are there so many fat demons?
Because they hate exorcising.

So I set up an internet page for Chinese Nazis..
So far it's gotten three Reichs on Facebook.

I saw on the news that the CEOs of T-mobile and Sprint got
married last weekend. Great wedding,
terrible reception.

Have you heard my paper joke?
It's tearable.

What do you call a broken can opener?
A can't opener.

What's Lil Wayne's favorite pizza?
Lil Seizures!

What do you call a fat psychic?
A four-chin teller!!
How does a penguin build his home?
Igloos it together.

A man just assaulted me with milk, butter and cheese
How dairy

Why are fish easy to weigh?

Because they have their own scales.

My drunk girlfriend asked me what I thought of her dancing
I told her it was just staggering.

What is the most well behaved drink?
Tea. Because the others are not tea

What's the police's favorite gaming console?
WII U WII U WII U WII U WII U WII U

I once swallowed two pieces of string and an hour later they
came out of my ass tied together.
I shit you knot.

RELIGIOUS

An Arab man is walking his animals when out of nowhere Jesus appears. Jesus walks up to the Arab man and asks, "Hi, good man. Could I speak to your dog?" The man replies, "Jesus, my dog can't speak." Jesus ignores the comment and addresses the dog. "Dog, how are you doing? Are you treated fairly?" The dog replies, "My lord, I am very happy. My owner feeds my well, walks me 3 times a day, and plays with me all the time." The Arab man stands there in astonishment. Jesus asks, "My good man, could I now speak to your horse?" The man replies, "Jesus, my horse can not speak." Jesus still addresses the horse. "Great beast, how are you, are you treated well?" The horse replies, "My lord, I am a might happy horse. I am walked and trained many times a day, fed very well, my hair is always combed, and all is good." At this point the man is at loss for words. Then Jesus asks, "My man, may I speak to your goat?" The man yells out, "NO, NOT THE GOAT, THE GOAT IS A LIAR."

The Pope and Trump are on stage in front of a huge crowd. The Pope leaned towards Mr. Trump and said, "Do you know that with one little wave of my hand I can make every person in this crowd go wild with joy? This joy will not be a momentary display, like that of your followers, but go deep into their hearts and for the rest of their lives whenever they speak of this day, they will rejoice!"
Trump replied, "I seriously doubt that. With one little wave of your hand? Show me!"
So the Pope slapped him

Why do Jews get Circumcised?
Because Jewish women refuse to touch anything that isn't at least 10% off.

A man gets on a bus, and ends up sitting next to a very attractive nun. Enamored with her, he asks if he can have sex with her. Naturally, she says no, and gets off the bus. The man goes to the bus driver and asks him if he knows of a way for him to have sex with the nun. "Well," says the bus driver, "every night at 8 o'clock, she goes to the cemetery to pray. If you dress up as God, I'm sure you could convince her to have sex with you." The man decides to try it, and dresses up in his best God costume. At eight, he sees the nun and appears before her. "Oh, God!" she exclaims. "Take me with you!" The man tells the nun that she must first have sex with him to prove her loyalty. The nun says yes, but tells him she prefers anal sex. Before you know it, they're getting down to it, having nasty, grunting, loud sex. After it's over, the man pulls off his God disguise. "Ha, ha! I'm the man from the bus!" "Ha, ha!" says the nun, removing her costume. "I'm the bus driver!"

Jesus once said "He who lives by the sword, will die by the sword"
He was a carpenter that died by being nailed to a piece of wood, so he might have had a point.

Science built skyscrapers and airplanes.
But only religion can bring the two together.

I was recently asked if I believed faith could move mountains. Apparently "No, but I've seen what it can do to buildings," is the wrong answer.

A boy is loudly praying, "God please give me a bicycle." His mom asks, "Why are you praying so loudly? God isn't hard of hearing." The boy replies, "Yes but grandma is."

Why doesn't Jesus trust mankind?
Because he's afraid they'll double-cross him.

Someone knocked on my door and asked if I had found Jesus. I explained it wasn't my turn to watch him this time, and they really should have used bigger nails.

There are three truths in religion:
1) Jewish people do not recognize Jesus as the Messiah.
2) Protestants do not recognize the Pope as the leader of the Christian faith.
Baptists don't recognize each other in the liquor store.

Noah lets all the animals off the ark and tells them, "Go forth, and multiply."
A year later, he goes around to all the animals to see how they're doing. The horses have foals, the wolves have pups, the lions have cubs...everything looks good. But then he gets to a couple of snakes, and they have no eggs, no hatch-lings, nothing.
Noah is confused, and the snakes admit that they've had some trouble.

"Is there anything I can do to help?" he asks.

The snakes look at each other, and then turn back to Noah. "If you could cut down that tree over there," says one, "that would help quite a bit."

Noah doesn't quite understand, but cuts down the tree anyway, and leaves to continue his journey. A year later, he goes to check the progress of all the animals. The are more foals, more pups, more cubs, and tons of other baby animals. He gets to the snakes, and sure enough, there are baby snakes everywhere.

Confused, Noah goes to one of the original snakes and asks how cutting down the tree helped.

"We're adders," said the snake. "We need logs to multiply."

Three nuns die and go to heaven. They arrive at the gates of heaven where they meet St. Peter who says "You must each answer one question about religion to enter heaven."

St. Peter calls the first nun and asks "who was the first man on Earth?" "Adam", she replies. So birds are chirping, angels are singing, the gates open, and she gets into heaven.

St. Peter asks the second nun, "Who was the first woman on Earth?" "Eve", she replies. So birds are chirping, angels are singing, the gates open, and she gets into heaven.

St. Peter asks the third nun, "What is the first thing Eve said to Adam?" The nun panics for a second because she doesn't know the answer. "Boy that's a hard one", she nervously replies. So birds are chirping, angels are singing, the gates open, and she gets into heaven.

A Muslim is about to commit suicide when a Catholic priest stops him.

"What are you doing?!" Exclaims the priest

"There is nothing on this Earth for me." The Muslim says, "I will commit suicide to go to paradise and get 72 virgins!"

The priest shakes his head.

"Foolish Muslim, suicide is not the way!" He says.

"Follow me, Ill take you to the local primary school."

So many Christians run non-profit organizations. On the other hand, atheists...

...only run non-prophet organizations.

A Jewish father was troubled by the way his son turned out, and went to see his Rabbi about it. "I brought him up in the faith, gave him a very expensive Bar Mitzvah, it cost me a fortune to educate him. Then he tells me last week he has decided to be a Christian! Rabbi, where did I go wrong?"

"Funny you should come to me," said the Rabbi. "Like you, I too, brought my boy up in the faith, put him through University, costs me a fortune, then one day, he too, tells me he has decided to become a Christian."

"What did you do?" asked the father.

"I turned to God for the answer", replied the Rabbi.

"And what did he say?" pressed the father.

"God said, 'Funny you should come to me...' "

An old German man goes to a priest for confession. When the priest slid open the panel in the confessional, the man said:

"Forgive me father, for I have sinned. During World War II, a beautiful Jewish woman, from our neighborhood, knocked urgently on my door and asked me to hide her from the Nazis. So I hid her in my attic."

The priest replied: "That was a wonderful thing you did. That's not a sin, and you have no need to confess that."

"There is more, Father. She started to repay me with sexual favors. This happened several times a week, and sometimes TWICE on Sundays."

The priest said, "That was a long,long time ago, and doing what you did placed the two of you in great danger. Two people under those circumstances can easily succumb to the weakness of the flesh. However, if you are truly sorry for your actions, you are indeed forgiven."

"Thank you, Father. That's a great load off my mind. It's good to know that I haven't done anything unforgivable, I do have one more question though."

"And what is that?" asked the priest.

"Should I tell her the war is over?"

A Buddhist monk goes to a barber to have his head shaved. "What should I pay you?" the monk asks. "No price, for a holy man such as yourself," the barber replies. And, what do you know, the next day the barber comes to open his shop, and finds on his doorstep a dozen gemstones. That day, a priest comes in to have his hair cut. "What shall I pay you, my son?" "No price, for a man of the cloth, such as yourself." And, what do you know, the next day the barber comes to open his shop, and finds on his doorstep a dozen roses. That day, Rabbi Finklestein comes in to get his payoss [sideburns] trimmed. "What do you want I should pay you?" "Nothing, for a man of God such as yourself." And the next morning, what do you know? The barber finds on his doorstep – a dozen rabbis.

A Mormon was seated next to an Irishman on a flight from London to the US.

After the plane was airborne, drink orders were taken. The Irishman asked for a whiskey, which was promptly brought and placed before him.

The flight attendant then asked the Mormon if he would like a drink. He replied in disgust, "I'd rather be savagely raped by a dozen whores than let liquor touch my lips."

The Irishman then handed his drink back to the attendant and said, "Me, too, I didn't know we had a choice."

In a small town in America, a person decided to open up his bar business, which was right opposite to a church. The church and its congregation started a campaign to block the bar from opening with petitions, and prayed daily against his business. Work progressed. However, when it was almost complete and was about to open a few days later, lightning struck the bar and it was burnt to the ground. The church folk were rather smug in their outlook after that, until the bar owner sued the church authorities for $2million, on the grounds that the church, through its congregation & prayers, was ultimately responsible for the demise of his bar shop, either through direct or indirect actions or means. In its reply to the court, the church vehemently denied all responsibility or any connection that their prayers were reasons to the bar shop's demise. In support of their claim they referred to the Benson study at Harvard that inter-cessionary prayer had no impact! As the case made its way into court, the judge looked over the paperwork and at the hearing and commented, 'I don't know how I am going to decide this case, but it appears from the paperwork, we have a bar owner who believes in the power of prayer and we have an entire church and its devotees that doesn't.'

Did you hear about the nun who procrastinated doing her laundry?
She had a filthy habit.

A man couldn't conceive so he prayed to God.
He asked God: "God please give me a child. It's all in the world I would ever want and the one thing I ask of you. If it's a boy, let him be a thief. If it's a girl let her be a cunt."
Just please Dear Lord grant me a child I may raise and love.
And so God granted him his wish, and soon his wife became with child and gave him a baby boy. And the father was happy, and raised him as best he could.
18 years later the child came to the father and said: "Father, you have raised me well and I wish to succeed in life, so I have decided to become a lawyer. "
The father leaves and goes straight to church and yells: "God I said a thief OR a cunt NOT BOTH!!!"

DIRTY

A man sunbathes in the nude and ends up burning his penis. His doctor tells him to ease the pain by dipping it in a saucer of cold milk. Later, his blonde wife comes home and finds him with his dick in a saucer of cold milk. "Good heavens!" she remarks "I always wondered how you reloaded those things!"

I like the smell of mothballs.
But it can sometimes be hard getting their little legs apart.

My favorite sex position is the WOW.
That's when I flip your MOM over.

My Indian GF said I could give her a facial...
I nearly came on the spot!

Jokes for the Modern Age

I told my boyfriend I wanted to try something I saw in a porno.
He wasn't as enthusiastic when I started fucking the pizza guy.

What did the two tampons say to each other?
Nothing. They were both stuck up cunts.

Whoever decided to name girl underwear "panties" fucked up.
How do you skip Cuntainers?

A blond woman goes to the hospital...
"What seems to be the problem?" asked the Doctor.
"Something is terribly wrong, I keep finding postage stamps from Costa Rica in my vagina."
The Doctor had a look, chuckled and said, "Those aren't postage stamps my dear, they're the stickers off the bananas."

Johnny the 5th grader needs to take a piss.
Johnny says to his teacher, "Ms. Hill can I go take a piss?"
Ms. Hill says, "Johnny, that's not appropriate language for a 5th grader. The proper word to use is urinate. Now, before you go to the bathroom.. use it in a sentence"
Johnny replied, "Urinate, but you'd be a 10 if you had bigger tits."

My dick may be only 4 inches...
But it smells like a foot.

How do you get an apple pregnant?

Jokes for the Modern Age

You cum in cider.

Life is like a penis.
It's all relaxed freely hanging, and then a woman comes and makes it hard.

A single sperm has 37.5 MB of DNA information in it. That means an average ejaculation represents a data transfer of 1587.5 TB.
That's a lot of information to swallow

What's the difference between a rook and a bishop?
Rooks can only move in straight lines, whereas bishops have sex with kids.

What's 10 inches long, hard as a rock, full of semen and makes all of the ladies scream?
The sock under my bed.

Why is the area between a woman's chest and hips called a waist?
Because you could easily fit another pair of tits in there.

If a blind girl ever tells you that you have a big penis, she's probably just pulling your leg.

Two deaf people get married, and during the first week of marriage, they find that they are unable to communicate in the bedroom with the lights out since, they can't see each other signing, or read lips. After several nights of fumbling around, and many misunderstandings, the wife figures out a

151

solution. She writes a note to her husband: 'Honey, Why don't we agree on some simple signals? For instance, at night, if you want to have sex with me, reach over and squeeze my left breast one time. If you don't want to have sex, reach over and squeeze my right breast two times. The husband thinks this is a great idea. He writes back to his wife that if she wants to have sex with him, reach over and pull on his penis one time. If she doesn't want to have sex, pull on his penis two hundred and fifty times.

I've discovered I have a logic fetish.
I can't stop coming to conclusions.

What do tofu and a dildo have in common?
They are both meat substitutes.

So I met a girl in the bar last night.
She said, "I haven't had a cock for nearly 2 weeks now"
So I took her back to my place and we started fooling around.
We got undressed and that's when I noticed the scars from the operation.

A guy and a girl go on a date and things get along so well that they decide to go to the girl's place...
Some flirting and fooling around later, the guy takes off his shirt, and then washes his hands.
He then takes off his trousers, and again washes his hands.
Watching all this the girl says, "You must be a dentist."
The guy, surprised, replies, "Why yes actually. How did you figure that out?" "Easy," she says, "you keep washing your hands."

One thing leads to another and they make love.
After it's over the girl says, "You must be a good dentist."
The guy, now with an inflated ego, "Sure - I'm a good dentist.
How did you figure that out?" To which she responds,
"Didn't feel a thing."

A husband had to leave his wife for 3 months while he
attended business in Africa. To prevent her loneliness and to
lower the temptations of her being unfaithful he went to the
local sex shop and asked the lady at the counter what the best
product she had to offer was. The woman pointed at the $400
sex doll in the corner and asked the man, "Will that do?" Not
wanting his wife to think of the sex doll as another man, the
husband shook his head and asked for another suggestion.
The counter clerk pointed at the back wall where a rack of
dragon dildos hung, to which the man replied that he had
plenty of those at home and was looking for something a little
more special.
Looking partially defeated, the counter clerk put her hand to
her forehead and thought for a while before removing her
hand and saying, "We have one other option but I really
wanted it for myself. It's one of a kind." The man, intrigued,
says, "Let me see it." The clerk pulls out a antiquated box
inlaid with gems along its side. She opens it and pulls out a
rather normal looking dildo and turns to the man, who is
obviously disappointed. The clerk sees this and announces,
"This is not just any old dildo. It's a magic dildo. It will fill
your wife with pleasure once she says the words, 'Magic
Dildo,' followed by whatever hole she desires to put it in. The
magic dildo will then fly up straight into her, filling her with
an orgasm like she's never had before. She'll be plenty busy

with it." The husband looks skeptical, so the clerk decides to display the dildo's powers for him. Holding the dildo in her hand, she confidently states "Magic dildo, my pussy." Upon which the dildo soars from her palm to her vagina, making her immediately open her mouth wide, in pants and intensity. After about ten minutes of this, she seems satisfied and says, "Magic dildo, the box." Making the dildo fly back to a rest. Impressed, the man rushes home to give the dildo to his wife.

A week after her husband left the wife decided to give the magic dildo a try. She left it in the garage and then went up into her bed and said, "Magic dildo, my pussy." Instantly it appeared where it was called and satisfied the wife. The wife was very excited about her magic dildo and started to use it every where. She called to it at work when no one was looking, in the wooded part of the park, at the movie theater, when she was dancing, everywhere. No matter where she was it would appear and make her squirm with pleasure.

One day, on her way to work the wife hit bad traffic. She looked up ahead and saw there was an accident and realized it would be a while, and decided to call the magic dildo. The wife was feeling really confident and called out, "Magic dildo, my pussy." She became overwhelmed and hit the accelerator slamming into the car in front of her. As it turned out that car was a cop.

The cop came up to the car seeing the woman squirming and suspected she was on drugs.

"Get out of the car now and put your hands on the hood!" The wife tried to comply but ended up just falling to the pavement. The officer was quite alright and asked the wife what she was on. The wife told him "Officer I'm not on any drugs, my husband gave me a magic dildo and its causing me to lose control!"

The officer, not buying it, simply replied, "Magic dildo, my ass."

A woman was in a long coma. A nurse was giving her a sponge bath, when she accidentally made contact with the woman's vagina, which produced a reaction on the heart monitor.

Excited, she went and told one of the Doctors, and he in turn called the woman's husband to tell him to come over as soon as possible.

"What's going on?" The husband asked, as he ran into the facility.

"Well sir, we found out that contact with your wife's privates elicits a response, and I feel that with the right stimulation she could be brought out of her coma."

"What do you suggest?" He asked with some excitement building.

"Well sir, I think some oral sex might be enough to get her back."

So the man agreed to it, and they left the room to give him some privacy with her, when not two minutes later, they here the monitor buzzing with a flat-line alert. The doctor runs in asking "what happened???"

The man shrugged and replied, "I guess she must have choked on it."

The other day I went to a Paraplegic Strip Club,
That place was crawling with pussy.

What's the best pick up line at a gay bar?
"May I push your stool in."

Son your teacher tells me you said the 'C' word in class today.
That wasn't clever was it?
No, it was cunt.

What's the difference between a joke and 4 dicks?
My ex can't take a joke.

How many dead hookers does it take to change a light bulb?
Apparently not three, because my basement is still dark.

A married couple of almost 20 years was lying in bed one evening. When the woman felt her husband begin to fondle her in ways he hadn't in quite some time. It almost tickled as his fingers started at her neck, and then began moving down past the small of her back. He then caressed her shoulders and neck, slowly worked his hand down over her breasts, stopping just over her lower stomach.
He then proceeded to place his hand on her left inner arm, caressed past the side of her breast again, working down her side, passed gently over her buttock and down her leg to her calf. Then, he proceeded up her inner thigh, stopping just at the uppermost portion of her leg. He continued in the same manner on her right side, then suddenly stopped, rolled over and became still. As she had become quite aroused by this caressing, she asked in a loving voice, "Honey that was wonderful. Why did you stop?"

Jokes for the Modern Age

"I found the remote," he mumbled.

My girlfriend didn't believe me when I said I have the body of 20 year old.
Her opinion changed when I opened the freezer.

What did the left cheek say to the right cheek?
If we stick together we can stop this shit.

What did a cannibal do after he dumped his girlfriend?
Wipe his ass.

Herb decided to propose to Jill, but prior to her acceptance, Jill felt she had to confess to her man that she suffered from a condition that left her breasts at the maturity of a 12 year old.
Herb said that it was okay because he loved her so much.
However, Herb felt this was also the time for him to open up and admit that he had a deformity, too.
Herb looked Jill in the eyes and said, "I too have a problem. My willy is the same size as a newborn, I hope you can deal with that once we are married."
She said, "Yes, I will marry you and learn to live with your newborn size willy."
Jill and Herb got married and they could not wait for the honeymoon. Herb whisked Jill off to their hotel suite and they started touching, teasing, and holding one another.
As Jill put her hands in Herb's pants, she began to scream and ran out of the room.
Herb ran after her to find out what was wrong.

She said, "You told me your willy was the size of a newborn infant!"
"Yes, it is…7 pounds, 8 ounces, and 17 inches long."

I was on a date, and I said, "You are the funniest and most beautiful woman I've ever met!"
She jokingly replied, "You just want to fuck me!"
"Wow!" I said, "Smart too!"

What do spinach and anal sex have in common?
If you were forced to have it as a kid, you're gonna hate it as an adult.

What should you do if your girlfriend starts smoking?
Slow down, and maybe use some lubricant.

Most colleges have a women's studies major, but mine has a men's studies major too.
It's called "history".

An exceptionally short, but good looking man was chatting up a tall, leggy blonde at a party.
Woman: "This is you're lucky night. I've never been with a midget and want to cross it off my list. Let's go back to my place."
Man: "Absolutely, just one thing. I can only have sex with the lights off."
She agrees and they go back to her place. There's just a bit of foreplay before he crawls down her, planting kisses along the

way. He gets between her legs and she feels the largest penis she's ever had in her life thrust into her.

Woman: "Oh God! That's so huge!"

Man: "If you like that, wait until I get the other leg in."

What's the difference between being hungry and being horny?
Where you put the cucumber.

I like my women like I like my cheesecake
Without someone else's dick in it you fucking bitch Victoria.

Women are like car parking spaces...
Usually, most of the good ones are taken. So once in a while, you gotta stick it in a disabled one.

So today my wife was screaming "Give it to me, I'm so wet! give it to me!"
She can scream all she wants, but the umbrella is mine.

I went out for a nice meal one day when the waiter asked, "How would you like your steak, sir?" "The same way I like my sex," I replied. He smiled and said, "So, rare?"

A woman is at home, when she hears someone knocking at her door. She goes to the door, opens it, and sees a man standing there. He asks the lady, "Do you have a Vagina?" She slams the door in disgust. The next morning she hears a knock at the door. Its the same man, and he asks the same question to the woman, "Do you have a Vagina?" She slams the door again. Later that night, when her husband gets home, she tells him what has happened for the last two days. The husband tells his wife in a loving and concerned voice, "Honey, I am taking an off tomorrow, so as to be home, just in case this guy shows up again." The next morning they hear a knock at the door and both ran for the door. The husband whispers to the wife, "Honey, I'm going to hide behind the door and listen, and if it is the same guy, I want you to answer yes to the question, because I want to a see where he's going with this." She nods yes to her husband and opens the door. Sure enough the same fellow is standing there. He asks, "Do you have a Vagina?" "Yes I do." says the lady. The man replies, "Good, would you mind telling your husband to leave my wife's alone and start using yours!"

Four Nuns traveling in a car get into an accident and die. They each arrive at the pearly gates where they are greeted by Saint Peter.

He tells them all that they've lived a good life and are welcome in, but only if they honestly answer his question. "Have you ever touched a penis since you became a Nun"? he asked the first one.

She thought hard and confessed, "Yes.... just once, with this finge.r"

"Very well, wash that finger in this bowl of holy water and you may enter".

He asked the second Nun, "Have you ever touched a penis since you became a Nun"?

She thought and said, "Yes...with this hand".

"Very well, wash your hand in the bowl and then you may enter".

He looks to the third Nun and says, "Have you ever tou....."

Just then, the fourth Nun pushes passed the third and says, "HEY, if you think I'm going to gargle that after she sticks her ass in it, you're fucking crazy".

I don't like the term 'Anal Bleaching'.
I prefer to call it 'changing my ringtone'.

In a way, good friends are like condoms...
...they protect you when things get hard.

A woman walks into Walmart. She's dragging her two children behind her and turns to yell at them, "Hurry up! Get your ass moving". The Walmart greeter can tell she's not having s good day, so he politely says, "Good morning, what a lovely day!" She rudely responds by telling the greeter to fuck off. The greeter is surprised, and asks her, "Ma'am are your two children twins?"
"Hell no, one is 5, the other is 8, and they don't look alike at all! Why the hell would you think they're twins?"
The greeter smiles and says, "I'm just having a hard time believing you got laid twice."

A married truck driver goes into a brothel. He says to the madam "I'll give you $500 for your ugliest girl and baked beans on burnt toast."
The madam replies "For $500 I'll give you my best looking girl and a 3 course meal."
The truck driver replies "You don't understand, I'm not horny, I'm homesick."

The Hardest Part About Breaking Up With A Japanese Girl?

You have to drop the bomb on her twice before she gets it.

Love is like a fart.
If you have to force it, it's probably shit.

A man was walking his dog through a graveyard when he
noticed a man crouching behind a gravestone.
"Morning!" He said.
Startled, the other man replies, "No, just having a shit."

A white man rubs on a genie bottle....
And the Genie comes out and says,
"Man, I've been in this damn bottle for 300 years, whatever
you want, you don't even have to say it, just think it and it'll
happen."
The man closes his eyes,
Bam! A mansion appears.
He closes his eyes again.
Bam! It becomes filled with beautiful, naked women.
He closes his eyes a third time.
Three men in white hoods knock on his door. He answers it,
they take him outside and hang him.
Later the genie is at the coffee shop talking to all the other
genies, and he says to his friends.
"Man I don't get it, the first wish is always the mansion, the
second wish is always women, but why on earth would this
man wish to be hung like a black man?"

If four people are having sex, it's a foursome. If three people
are having sex, it's threesome.

Jokes for the Modern Age

Finally I understand why people call me handsome.

How do you spot a blind man at a nudist colony?
It's not hard.

A penguin is driving when he sees a check engine light on. He takes his car to the mechanic and then goes for ice cream. He gets a big dish of ice cream and sits down to eat. Having no hands, he makes a real mess trying to eat. After finishing his ice cream, he goes back to the gas station and asks the mechanic if he's found the problem. The mechanic looks up and says, "It looks like you blew a seal." "No no," the penguin replies, "it's just vanilla ice cream."

Jokes that say women should stay in the kitchen are so offensive.
How else are they supposed to clean the rest of the house?

So I've been putting Viagra in my milk.
It doesn't help with the sex, but my Oreos don't go all soft anymore.

When a woman buys a vibrator it's seen as a bit of naughty fun. But when a guy orders a 240 volt fuckmaster pro 5000 latex doll with high speed pulsating pussy, elasticized anus with non drip semen collection tray, together with optional built in realistic orgasm sound system, he gets called a pervert.

The teacher was trying to avoid calling on Dirty Johnny, the most foul mouthed kid in third grade.

She asked Cindy to name a three syllable word and use it in a sentence, while Dirty Johnny waved his hand frantically.

"Beautiful. My teacher is beautiful" said Cindy.

"That's correct, and very sweet of you." the teacher replied.

Johnny was still waving his hand, but the teacher called on Derek.

"Wonderful. I have a wonderful teacher."

"Thank you Derek! Your answer is also correct."

Now only Dirty Johnny has his hand up. The teacher sighs and calls on him.

"Urinate!" Dirty Johnny exclaims.

The teacher is surprised. This isn't as bad as she expected...

"Urinate, but if you had bigger tits, you'd be a ten!"

What do you call a bunch of white guys sitting on a bench?
The NBA.

Where do suicide bombers go after they die?
Everywhere.

A man was having premature ejaculation problems so he went to the doctor. The doctor said, "When you feel like you are getting ready to ejaculate, try startling yourself." That same day the man went to the store and bought himself a starter pistol and ran home to his wife. That night the two were having sex and found themselves in the 69 position. The man felt the urge to ejaculate and fired the starter pistol. The next day he went back to the doctor who asked how it went. The man answered, "Not well. When I fired the pistol, my wife pooped on my face, bit three inches off my penis, and my neighbor came out of the closet with his hands in the air."

My german girlfriend likes to rate my sexual performances on a scale of 1-10.
Last night we tried anal. She kept yelling 9. That's the best I've ever done.

I wipe my butt the same way I drive.
Stop on red.

I went to a brothel and met a prostitute
I asked her what are the prices? She said:
$20 for a hand job.
$50 for a blow job.
$80 for sex.
And for $120, I'll do anything!
Anything? Hmmm....
She's now fitting my downstairs bathroom and repainting my living room.
You can get some real bargains if you shop around!

I found out my buddy had an acorn fetish
It's fucking nuts.

What do you call a woman that has sex for spaghetti?
A pastatute.

What's a man's most sensitive body part when he's masturbating in the bathroom?

His ears.

What does a perverted frog say?
Rub it, rub it.

I met a girl with a twelve nipples.
Sounds funny.
Dozen tit?

A man is being arrested by a female police officer, who informs him, "Anything you say can and will be held against you." The man replies, "Boobs!"

An 18-year-old Italian girl tells her mother that she has missed her period for the past two months.
Very worried, the mother goes to the drugstore and buys a pregnancy kit. The test result shows that the girl is pregnant. Shouting, cursing, crying, the mother says, "Who was the pig that did this to you? I want to know!"
The girl picks up the phone and makes a call. Half an hour later, a Ferrari stops in front of their house. A mature and distinguished man, with gray hair and impeccably dressed in an Armani, suit steps out of the of the Ferrari and enters the house.
He sits in the living room with the father, mother, and the girl and tells them, "Good morning. Your daughter has informed me of the problem. I can't marry her because of my personal family situation, but I'll take charge." "I will pay all costs and provide for your daughter for the rest of her life."
"Additionally, if a girl is born, I will bequeath a Ferrari, a beach house, two retail stores, a townhouse, a beachfront villa,

and a $2,000,000 bank account. If a boy is born, my legacy will be a couple of factories and a $4,000,000 bank account. If twins, they will receive a factory and $2,000,000 each. However, if there is a miscarriage, what do you suggest I do?"

At this point, the father, who had remained silent, places a hand firmly on the man's shoulder and tells him, "You fuck her again."

What did the kamikaze pilot tell his students?
Watch closely. I'm only gonna show this once.

What do you call a hooker's farts?
Prostitoots.

A trucker's wife sees 3 parrots for sale at $160, $150, and $10. She asks, "Why is the last parrot so cheap?!" and the store owner replied
"It used to live in a whore house."
So the woman laughs and buys the parrot and gets home. When she enters, the parrot says,
"WOW, a new whore house!"
Later, the woman's two daughters arrive and the parrot says,
"Damn! Two new gals just got hired!"
They all laugh and go to have dinner, which is when the father comes home. The parrot says,
"Hey, Dave! I see you found the new spot!"

My ex is like the Mona Lisa. It's not that she is pretty or anything, but I would be overjoyed if I came home to find her hanging in the living room.

Masturbating while looking in a mirror isn't wrong.
Unless it's a rear view mirror, and you're driving a school bus.